(06-13414) 7-24-69

THE CENTERS OF CIVILIZATION SERIES

Vienna in the Age of Franz Josef

Vienna

IN THE AGE OF FRANZ JOSEF

❧ ❧

Arthur J. May

UNIVERSITY OF OKLAHOMA PRESS : NORMAN

BY ARTHUR J. MAY

*Contemporary American Opinion of the Mid-Century
Revolutions in Central Europe* (Philadelphia, 1927)
Europe and Two World Wars (New York, 1947)
The Hapsburg Monarchy, 1867–1914 (Cambridge, 1960)
The Age of Metternick (New York, 1963)
*A History of Civilization since the Mid-Seventeenth
Century* (New York, 1964)
The Passing of the Hapsburg Monarchy
(Philadelphia, 1965)
Vienna in the Age of Franz Josef (Norman, 1966)

Library of Congress Catalog Card Number: 66–13414

Copyright 1966 by the University of Oklahoma Press, Publishing Division of the University. Composed and printed
at Norman, Oklahoma, U.S.A., by the University of
Oklahoma Press. First edition.

To
LYDIA, INGEBORG, *and* GRETL
who taught me much about Vienna

Preface

THE VIENNA of the Emperor Franz Josef stands out as a noble beacon—*la ville lumière*—in the heart of Europe. During his long reign the city was transformed from a relatively remote outpost of Western civilization into a metropolis of more than two millions, the capital in every sense of the Hapsburg Monarchy of fifty-one millions. The brilliant cosmopolitan culture that emerged, steadily nourished by fresh talents from outside, radiated in all directions, most importantly doubtless to the underdeveloped Near East, but also across the broad Atlantic.

This adventure in portraiture extends from the lilting waltzes of the elder Johann Strauss to the first cacophonies of Arnold Schönberg, from the romantic literary tastes of Franz Grillparzer to the cynical psychological realism and despairing pessimism, illuminated only fitfully by flashes of hope, of Arthur Schnitzler, from the quiet landscapes of Ferdinand G. Waldmüller to the erotic females painted by Egon Schiele, from the austere brick Altlerchenfeld church to the white marble gem of ecclesiastical architecture by Otto Wagner at the Am Steinhof asylum, from the assertive Catholicism of Cardinal Joseph O. von Rauscher to the psychoanalytical pinnacle of Sigmund Freud, from the dawn of the railway age to the first stage of the motor-car revolution, from the rule of authoritarianism in municipal administration toward political democracy, and from the tumultuous revolution of 1848 to the encircling gloom that attended the funeral of Franz Josef in the midst of the First World War.

Although the accent rests upon the creative, cultural, and intellectual glories of Vienna, the sweep of the narrative is broad and on this small canvas decidedly eclectic. If the Danubian metropolis was a city of dreams, it was likewise a city of contradictions. Swift urbanization, a fivefold increase of population within seventy years, created novel opportunities for the inner life, the culture of spirit and mind, but that expansion also raised new and formidable problems of municipal housekeeping—health and education, for example, and housing and transportation.

Other investigators wiser—or bolder—than the present writer have defined the character—the *mystique*—of the "Queen City" on the Danube and its inhabitants. That the community possessed something of a distinctive personality, reflecting the uninterrupted mingling of human stocks within its borders, is undeniable. On these subjects, a huge volume of polemical literature has accumulated. Many authors find the pattern of Vienna living in gaiety, charm, lightheartedness, in Strauss melodies, *Wiener Schnitzel*, and dashing cavaliers in surroundings of baroque opulence. Other analysts have been impressed by Viennese cheerfulness, tolerance, unfailing courtesy, and hospitality from prince to pauper, wit, humor, instinctive nostalgia for the past, and remarkable capacity for accepting catastrophes with stoical dignity. Nor may one overlook the image of a pleasure-loving Vienna, a romantic fairyland, portrayed by the Hollywood celluloid plutocracy.

It cannot be gainsaid that the qualities enumerated above were—are—detectable in the individual Viennese, but to erect glowing generalizations on foundations of that nature is not only highly imaginative and sentimental, but distorted, illusory, and mythological. The more ecstatic commentators on "the spirit of Vienna" resemble men who have fallen under the subtle spell of a seductive woman.

Let it be recognized, however, that Vienna was—is—a city of delight, rich in history and drama, in which any healthy person could—can—enjoy himself, and in which endless potentialities made boredom unthinkable. It was a city of work, a city of two nations—the glamor and ostentation of the wealthy few contrasting with the circumscribed existence of the disadvantaged—as well as a city of song, new wine, and the mausoleum of departed Hapsburgs lying in stately dignity beneath the church of the Capuchins.

My personal interest in Vienna stems from lifelong study of the Hapsburg Monarchy and the need for a substantial history of the capital in the English language. Residence in Vienna on eight occasions, for varying periods of time, have enabled me to acquire the "feel" of the community—however impossible to translate that fascination into defensible paragraphs. It was the poet Rainer Maria Rilke who wrote of Vienna that " . . . one cannot express what it is that makes its old streets so unique, its squares so old-fashioned, the old Hofburg with its courtyards so ceremonious and formal, the Ring so splendid, the gardens so ample, the baroque fountains so indispensable . . . ." On the other side, firsthand familiarity with the community is apt to interfere with that dispassionate, objective reconstruction to which the professional historian in Western society aspires.

For this work, my studies have ranged over press materials, municipal reports, Vienna archival records, accounts by travelers from abroad, as well as monographs and books. But readers will look in vain for footnotes revealing my indebtedness to men and women whose researches and suggestive insights have been drawn upon. Except for microscopic monographs, all writing about the past is inescapably a synthetic undertaking; the bibliography indicates the principal works that have been found most helpful.

To list the living Viennese who have contributed to my knowledge and understanding of their city would make a lengthy catalog, and it may seem invidious to acknowledge special obligations to University Dozent Rudolf Till, to Felix Czeike, both on the staff of the Vienna *Stadtarchiv*, and to the three ladies to whom the book is gratefully dedicated. An expression of gratitude is also due to the anonymous attendants in archival treasure houses and libraries in Vienna, London, Washington, D.C., Philadelphia, and Rochester, who have facilitated my labors.

With exemplary patience and skill, Mrs. Kenneth G. Kugler, of Rochester, New York, typed the manuscript.

Rochester, New York   Arthur J. May
November, 1965

Contents

Vienna in the Age of Franz Josef

∾ 1 ≈

Vienna in 1848

On Saturday, December 2, 1848, Franz Josef, a slim, good-looking, dignified young man of eighteen was crowned emperor of Austria, a realm of about thirty-eight million embracing a mélange of peoples, languages, customs, and creeds. Confronting the new monarch and his senior ministers was a sea of troubles, for earlier in 1848 historic bonds of loyalty and obedience to the house of Hapsburg, rooted traditions of order and discipline, had been ruptured. Large sections of the citizenry in the imperial capital, Vienna, had rebelled and rebelled again. Czech dissidents in Bohemian Prague had revolted and been subdued by cannon fire. Kindred outbreaks had severely shaken the Italian provinces of the realm and had been similarly repressed by arms. The kingdom of Hungary, seething with disaffection, was still in an uproar.

Born in 1830 at Laxenburg Castle near Vienna, Franz Josef was very definitely the child of his mother, the Archduchess Sophie of Bavaria. Clever and proud, she was endowed with a tenacious will and resolved to seat her son on the venerable throne of the Hapsburgs. Education of the young prince in the art of statecraft was entrusted to Klemens Metternich, chancellor of the empire, and in the Roman Catholic faith to Archbishop (later Cardinal) Josef

3

O. von Rauscher. He was thoroughly schooled in military affairs and reflected throughout his long life the stern virtues of the soldier. Tutors taught him a smattering of history and languages, and inculcated in him the political philosophy of the divine right of a monarch to rule.

Destiny decreed that the Austrian autocrat should preside over the multinationality realm for sixty-eight years, short of a few days—one of the longest reigns in Western annals. He acceded to the throne just as the railway age was being ushered in on the Continent, and he remained in power until after gasoline-powered vehicles had started transforming the habits of urban living in scores of directions. Put another way, Franz Josef entered the world when Andrew Jackson resided in the White House, took the imperial scepter during the Presidency of James K. Polk, and laid down his burdens a fortnight after Woodrow Wilson was elected to the Presidency a second time.

In the interval his capital city, his beloved Vienna, had experienced a radical reformation, advancing majestically from a somewhat remote outpost of the Western way of life in the heart of Europe to rival Paris among communities. Her men of science and scholarship, her architects and city planners, her virtuosos of music and the other fine arts, her novelists and poets, her dramatists and actors, relatively few of them Viennese in family origins, raised the "Queen of the Danube" to unexampled heights of distinction. Simultaneously, the transforming might of industrialism, capitalistic finance, a huge growth of population, and experimentation in municipal "socialism" had wrought powerfully upon the texture and quality of the city.

In a manner of speaking, the Vienna of 1848 comprised

three communities in one: the historic inner city, the *Altstadt*, surrounded by fortifications, the suburban districts beyond with a second series of walls at their edge, and, finally, the fringing clusters of villages, vineyards, and woodlands. The ancient brick ramparts around the inner city, austere and rising to a height of more than fifty feet, advertised the medieval, or provincial, character of Vienna. However serviceable the walls had once been in warding off the hosts of Islamic Turkey, they had lost their relevance in the Europe of the nineteenth century. Twice the armies of Napoleon had stormed in almost at will, and on their second withdrawal in 1809, the French troops blew up a section of the old battlements.

On top of the bastions ran a promenade, extending for more than three miles, with trees, benches, and coffee-houses replacing cannon, and on fair Sundays after Mass the esplanade was thronged to the point of congestion. Splendid vistas of the suburban districts and the picturesque countryside rewarded pedestrians. Eight gates, closed promptly at ten in the evening, penetrated the massive walls and admitted wayfarers through dark, tunnel-like passages to the inner city. Bridges in front of each gate crossed a tree-planted moat, and beyond stretched a glacis, varying from fifty-five to a little more than one hundred yards, with a labyrinth of paths and gardens and a parade ground for the public or for army maneuvers.

The first tier of suburbs reached off to a second girdle of ramparts, the *Linienwall*, which when finished in 1704 enclosed almost the entire Vienna of that day. Built for defense, the walls rose to twelve feet, and they had eleven gates, and a ditch in front. At the entrances tolls were collected on consumer-goods, fuel included, brought into the city; all concerned chafed under these payments, and smuggling was rife. Placid agricultural hamlets, vineyards, the Vienna woods, and pleasant mountain spurs covered the outer suburban region.

Leopoldstadt, the most populous of the suburbs, occupied the left bank of the Danube Canal. It contained busy commercial quarters, fish-selling sheds on floats at the water's edge, and entertainment resorts—such as the sumptuous Diana public bath, for instance, which in winter was fitted up for dancing. Here, too, was a large prison, a model of its kind and much visited by foreigners interested in penal institutions. Close by the Leopoldstadt was the expanding industrial village of Florisdorf.

At the mid-nineteenth century the suburbs of Vienna, in which resided nearly 300,000 souls, were about five times more populous than the inner city. In them were located small shops and mills, many of recent construction, and the dwelling places of the proletariat. Suburban Alsergründ was the site of the vast General Hospital and other facilities for medical care. Covering twenty-four acres, the hospital contained about three thousand beds, and in the spacious grounds a dozen courtyards, prettily shrubbed, were laid out. By the standards of the time, the hospital was well constructed, though badly ventilated, and bulky stoves furnished warmth in winter. Clinics, normally overcrowded, afforded unexcelled opportunities for training medical students. Inside the compound was a lying-in-hospital where pregnant, unwed women could repair with no questions asked; if a mother desired, her child could be turned over to a nearby foundling hospital.

An insane asylum likewise stood within the area of the General Hospital—a grotesque structure, five stories in

6

height, having the shape of a round tower. Patients, who might number as many as three hundred, were chained as though they were wild beasts and on occasion beaten and exhibited to curious onlookers of a sadistic turn of mind.

Not far away was the Josephinum, an institution founded toward the end of the eighteenth century primarily to train medical men to care for the fighting services, with a well-managed hospital attached. It was equipped with a magnificent library and several museums, one holding an extraordinary collection of wax anatomical preparations. Attended by upwards of three hundred students, the Josephinum had an enviable international reputation as a training center for medicine and surgery.

Apart from being the home of shopkeepers, mill workers, and civil servants, the suburbs were dotted with grand palaces, exquisitely mirroring the stately existence of the imperial household and of the more élite aristocratic families. Noblest of them all was Schönbrunn, summer residence of the Hapsburg dynasty and the headquarters of Napoleon while his soldiers garrisoned Vienna. Two wings flanked the central block of the cream-colored palace, which had more than fourteen hundred rooms, one in ten of them a kitchen. A suite of apartments, once the quarters of servants, was remodeled in a gay and tasteful manner as a restaurant to which the public was welcomed on Sunday.

On weekends, when the weather permitted, Viennese commoners streamed through the park and formal gardens of Schönbrunn, occupying more than five hundred acres. Hedges of tall trees, clipped to look like canyons, concealed niches in which sculptured figures were set on pedestals. Broad footpaths led past fountains, an artificial lake, a tiny spring (*Brunn*), which gave the estate its name, artificial ruins, and choice displays of flowers. Graveled walks ascended to a terraced hilltop on which was perched a purely ornamental *Gloriette,* an arcaded pavilion more than one hundred yards in length. From this eminence the old Hapsburg capital in the distance could be seen to great advantage.

A second suburban hill was crowned by the principal mansion of the Belvedere complex, erected early in the eighteenth century as the summer residence of Prince Eugene of Savoy, ablest of Hapsburg military captains. It was subsequently acquired by the state and converted into a gallery for the imperial collection of paintings, especially of the Flemish and German schools. Stretching away from this excellent specimen of baroque residential architecture were spacious, carefully manicured French gardens, generously provided with tall green hedges, pieces of sculpture, and fountains; at the northern extremity the rambling, two-story Lower Belvedere housed a remarkable assemblage of trophies from the Turkish wars—armor and weapons, instructive alike from an artistic viewpoint and as depicting the evolution of the tools of war. Botanical gardens of the University of Vienna, which bordered the Belvedere property, provided opportunities for observation and study.

Impressive, too, was the huge, oval-shaped Schwarzenberg Palace with flanking wings and handsome gardens. And even more note-worthy was the summer mansion of the princely Liechtenstein family in the Rossauer district. The marble entrance was breath-taking in its proportions, and a superb staircase and wonderful frescoes and ceiling paintings imparted special distinction to the dwelling. But the supreme glory was room upon room of works of art, chiefly paintings by Rubens, Vandyke, and Frans Hals, though not by them alone. Altogether the Liechtenstein treasures formed perhaps the richest private gallery in existence and compared favorably with many government-owned collections in other European cities. Like the gallery, the surrounding gardens were open to visitors.

Across the glacis from the Burg gate stood yet another solid and sumptuous pile, the Palace of the Hungarian Guards, in which normally sixty young men of Hungarian noble extraction received training for war and in the social graces. On ceremonial occasions, the Hungarian Guards attended the emperor, decked out in colorful scarlet costumes embroidered with silver lace; tiger skins hung from the shoulders of the youths in this exotically colorful band, and they wore tall fur caps with flowing heron plumes.

Outside the walls, too, was a majestic church, the *Karlskirche*, or Charles Church, erected in the early eighteenth century in thanksgiving for the deliverance of Vienna from plague and honoring the sacred memory of Saint Carlo Borromeo, an eminent prelate of Milan, venerated both for his zealous labors in the Catholic Reformation and for exemplary service to his flock during a virulent epidemic of 1576. Designed in the exuberant baroque style then in fashion, the central portion of the church façade featured a Corinthian portico with six columns reminiscent of classical temples; at each side of the portico a towering column resembled the well-known monument of Trajan in Rome and niches for bells occupied the corners. Surmounting all was a sculptured representation of Saint Carlo above a bas-relief depicting the cessation of the death-dealing plague. Inside the oval sanctuary paintings

9

showed the saint entering heaven and illustrated other themes having Christian implications.

Not far away was a Technological College, opened in 1818, and dedicated by Emperor Francis II to "intellectual growth for the common good of my beloved and faithful burgher classes." The structure impressed an observant American as "about as large as all the buildings of Yale or Harvard thrown together." Outstanding collections of technical materials for teaching purposes were available, and student personnel in the several divisions of technology approached the two-thousand mark. In the same general suburban area was a small but excellent college of veterinary medicine, under the University of Vienna administration. On the secondary level of education there was the historic Theresianum, an academy established in a former imperial villa, where about 170 aristocratic boys underwent training for state service over a twelve year period. Another suburb boasted an exclusive secondary school conducted by Piaristen fathers.

Many streets in suburban Vienna were merely bare soil, sandy and loose, which strong winds recurrently whipped into clouds of dust thick enough to obscure the inner city, and rain reduced to seas of mud. Five wooden bridges, rickety enough in all likelihood, linked the suburb across the Danube Canal with the city proper.

Historians of Vienna have sometimes neglected the growing, populous suburban districts and concentrated on the area inside the medieval walls, barely a mile across. There the imperial palace (Hofburg) was located, as well as many aristocratic residences, government offices, ancient churches, educational institutions, and shops of every description.

Since the late thirteenth century a complex of structures, interspersed with courtyards, known as the Hofburg, or Burg, served as the principal quarters of Hapsburg dynasts. A conglomeration of architectural styles, the Hofburg was repeatedly altered, extended, or reconstructed over a span of almost six hundred years. The Hofburg, consisting of seventeen different buildings, was constructed in seventeen different ages and in seventeen different styles, someone wryly observed. Within, the private apartments of the imperial family were plain but comfortable, and the music and ball rooms possessed regal grandeur. Across the way, beyond walls and glacis, the very fine imperial stables housed hundreds of horses, handsome carriages, and sleighs embellished with gold and sable, some of which had seats fifteen feet above the ground, to be drawn by two or four horses.

A section of the Hofburg housed the Imperial Library— "a temple worthy of the intellectual treasures it enshrined." Over the generations some 300,000 volumes had been accumulated, together with a mass of rare manuscripts and incunabula of the fourteenth to sixteenth centuries, specially lodged in a commodious room. Books and folios which were once the property of Prince Eugene of Savoy occupied another section. Facilities for readers—the resources had been available to the general public since 1726—were quite limited. In the magnificent baroque great hall, perhaps the finest room of its kind in the world, rows of multicolored books in morocco bindings filled richly ornamented cases; portraits and statues of benefactors and incomparable globes enhanced the impressiveness of this spacious central room.

Adjoining the library was the imperial museum of

natural history exhibiting very large collections of animals, birds, and fish, as well as a bizarre assembly of mice, all skillfully arranged. Landscape paintings, illustrating the scenery of the portion of the globe of which a given animal or bird was native, decorated the walls.

Within easy walking distance were the baroque Ballhaus, the working quarters of Chancellor Metternich and the offices of the ministry of foreign affairs; there the formal sessions of the historic Congress of Vienna at the end

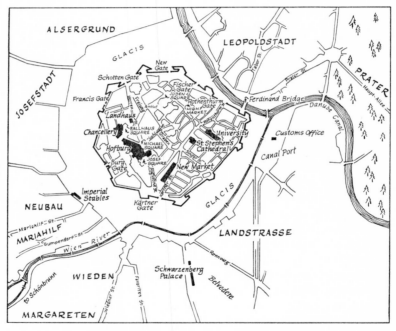

Vienna at the Accession of Franz Josef

of the Napoleonic wars had been conducted. Municipal administration was conducted in the nearby city hall, most of which dated from the eighteenth century, though parts were five hundred years old; for over twenty generations this center had been intimately identified with events in Viennese annals. So solidly was the building constructed that it promised to last for generations to come, though the layout was antiquated, having been designed for a smaller city in less busy and less complex centuries.

Picturesque baroque mansions encrusted with florid

Vienna, the Inner City

13

ornamentation and the property of great patrician families of the realm abounded in the inner city. The largest of the palaces was the former winter residence of Prince Eugene of Savoy, used in 1848 as a government mint and in a later age taken over by the national ministry of finance. A majestic staircase, lavishly decorated ceilings, a balustrade supported by eighteen sculptured sons of Hercules lent a special quality to this baroque masterpiece. Duke Albert of Sachsen-Teschen assembled in his grand palace an extraordinary array of graphic prints and drawings.

The higher learning was cultivated in the University of Vienna—Alma Mater Rudolfina—dating from 1365, by the faculties of philosophy, law, medicine, and theology. Designed in French classic style, the imposing university edifice presented a somewhat gloomy appearance, and lecture halls were small and poorly laid out. A staff of eighty professors lectured to about two thousand ordinary students and almost as many more "irregulars"; the internationally renowned Vienna medical school enrolled nearly as many learners as the other two professional faculties, law and theology, combined. Lesser institutions of mature learning in the city included a commercial college and a unique Oriental Academy, which specialized in equipping young men for the diplomatic service, preference in admission being granted to sons of noble families. Instruction in the fine arts, in music, and in pedagogy was offered in separate academies.

Outstanding among secondary schools was the Schotten Gymnasium, catering to boys of nine to fourteen years of age and teaching the classical languages and literatures, history and religion, and a bit of geography and mathematics. All told, Vienna in 1848 had some seventy elementary schools which imparted the four R's—reading and writing, arithmetic and religion—to about twenty-eight thousand pupils. Instruction was carried on in classes numbering about one hundred, and the master was helped by a corps of assistants. Without exception, schools were thoroughly disciplined and permeated with Catholic-oriented approaches to the good life.

Fees had to be paid for all pupils save orphans or children of serving soldiers. For the most part, female religious societies, notably the reformed Ursulines, bore responsibility for teaching girls from households of wealth and status.

Quite likely the rate of literacy in Vienna matched that of any other city of Western Europe, except Berlin—approximately 10 per cent of the boys of appropriate age studied in secondary schools. At all levels educational institutions were closely linked to the Roman Catholic Church and supervised by clerics and civil officials, who had even to approve books that were used in teaching. For the time, Vienna charitable institutions, some fifty in all, cared rather well for foundlings and orphans, for the blind, deaf, and dumb, and for the aged sick and infirm. The major prison in the *Altstadt*, however, had a vile reputation for overcrowding and shackling inmates when they were not engaged in manual labor.

Vienna inside the walls teemed with elegant, architecturally diversified churches, but the venerable Cathedral of St. Stephen—symbolic landmark of the city—was always the most magnificent. Begun in the thirteenth century on the site of an older Christian edifice, this essentially Gothic structure with certain Romanesque touches had been many times renovated and embellished. The noble spire seemed almost detached from the rest of the church; two-thirds of the way up, a platform served as a watchtower in time of external danger and as a station for fire wardens, who in daytime rang a bell and hoisted a red flag if a fire was detected and at night placed a light in the direction in which a fire had broken out. According to police regulations, every substantial residential building had to have a well, leathern pails, and a ladder for use in case of fire. When an alarm was signaled from St. Stephen's, fire wardens on streets beat drums and commandeered pedestrians to fight the blaze and carts to haul water.

Because the nave lacked upper lights and windows were few, the interior of the Cathedral was dark, and it was rendered the dingier by an accumulation of dust and dirt generations old. All day long worshipers or mere sightseers walked by picturesque baroque altars and side chapels and gazed at statues and other monuments of ecclesiastical and political celebrities or at paintings and pieces of sculpture illustrating one facet or another of the Christian heritage. On special occasions, holy relics belonging to St. Stephen's were displayed on the high altar—a fragment of Christ's linen girdle and a strip of the cloth that covered the table at the Last Supper. In catacombs beneath the sanctuary, corpses were thrown together in hideous and horrifying mounds.

Customarily, the Hapsburg court heard Mass in the plain, Gothic Augustiner Church, which was connected to the Hofburg by a private passageway. Hearts of Hapsburgs of an earlier age were preserved—and displayed—in silver jars in the adjoining Loretto chapel. Much praised was a coldly beautiful cenotaph, suggestively pagan, chiseled as a memorial to Maria Christina, a daughter of Empress Maria Theresa, by the Italian sculptor, Antonio

Canova. In form a pyramid of marble, the monument showed weeping youths bearing torches like Greek athletes, while Charity led up a tottering old man and a boy to the tomb before which waited a youthful personification of death; female figures displayed rare delicacy of expression and womanly loveliness.

Scores of Hapsburgs rested in sarcophagi in a crypt underneath the baroque Capuchin Church, impressive in its simplicity and austerity. Old custom prescribed that the coffins should be made of wood with metal outer shells. Some of the caskets were in fact works of art; those holding the remains of emperors, empresses, and their children were covered with black velvet and gold ornamentation, but lesser members of the imperial family had to be content with silver decoration and red velvet. By decree of Joseph II, coffins were to be simple unadorned copper boxes, and that fashion prevailed until the interment of the Archduchess Sophie (1872), mother of Franz Josef, whose casket was luxuriantly ornamented. The vault was the final resting place of only a single commoner—a favorite governess of Maria Theresa. For a fee, long-bearded Capuchin brothers, torchlight in hand, guided curious visitors around this receptacle of departed imperial grandeur.

At the side of the University structure was a garishly decorated Jesuit church, notable for ceiling paintings and oddly twisted pillars and statues of imitation marble. On an elevation above the Danube Canal stood a small, unprepossessing Ruprecht church, reputedly the oldest in Vienna, Romanesque portions of it dating from early in the thirteenth century. Frequented by a fashionable clientele was the fine old Michaeler Church, incorporating Romanesque and Gothic tastes, whose porch was distinguished by a remarkable representation in stone of the Archangel Michael. Princely tombs of artistic significance and a chaste baroque high altar loomed up in the dark interior.

As witness to the cosmopolitan character of the Viennese population, preaching in several churches during the Lenten season was done in foreign tongues. Magyar was spoken in the Malteser Church, dedicated to St. John the Baptist, Italian in the dull Gothic Minoriten Church, Polish in the Salvator chapel adjoining the city hall, and French in little St. Anne's. Czechs worshipped at Maria am Gestade, small, but an architectural gem, Gothic in part. The nave was lofty, singularly narrow, and had no aisles; the choir was turned on a curious oblique angle, and a fine tower, variously shaped, culminated in elaborate fretwork.

Nearly a score of monastic establishments existed in the Vienna of 1848, thirteen of them for men. Most impressive was the vast Schotten monastery and church of the Benedictine order, a community in itself, founded by monks from the British Isles, who were subsequently replaced by Germans; the famous Schotten school for boys has been noticed earlier. The monastery and church of the sons of St. Francis blended in an interesting fashion late Gothic and Renaissance architectural styles.

The small company of Viennese who worshipped in the traditions of Martin Luther or John Calvin, mainly comfortably fixed business and professional families, met in downtown churches standing side by side in a former Catholic convent. Communicants of Orthodox Eastern Christianity maintained at least four chapels, and Jews had two or three temples, a synagogue of the reformed version of the faith being "not without some pretensions to elegance."

Like the fortifications and many public buildings, the warren of streets in the inner city, narrow, crooked, and paved with large stones, harked back to the Middle Ages. Vienna had grown up helter-skelter without any semblance of planning. "It needs a weasel's wisdom," commented an American visitor, "to thread the dark and winding passages," which, if wet, were muddy and treacherous. Street lighting with gas was introduced in the 1840's by an English company, but the beam from lamps was slight and the performance uncertain. Before ten o'clock in the evening streets were practically deserted, except for patrons of amusement, resorts, or chance roisterers.

A corps of about seven hundred men constituted the entire police force in city and suburbs. Watchmen prowled about at night in gray frock coats, large tin hats, long leathern aprons, black gaiters, and baskets slung over their shoulders. They carried formidable iron-tipped poles with which they struck the pavement when church clocks announced the passing hour, and sang appropriately:

> *Good people all, I pray take care,*
> *And speedily to bed repair,*
> *For midnight strikes, the day expires,*
> *So shut your doors and quench your fires.*

By day, foreigners of many origins and tongues invested the central streets with exotic color—and strong odors. To an American traveler Vienna seemed "like a fancy ball. Hungarians, Poles, Croats, Wallachians, Jews, Moldavians, Greeks, Turks, all dressed in their national and striking costumes, promenade up and down, smoking all . . . . Every third window is a pipe-shop, and they show by their splendor and variety the expensiveness of the passion. Some [pipes] are marked 'Two hundred dollars.' The streets reek with tobacco smoke. You never catch a breath of untainted air within the Glacis. Your hotel, your cafe, your coach, your friend are all redolent of the same disgusting odour."

Pleasing monuments or fountains adorned many of the city's charming squares and quaint courtyards. Before the Imperial Library, for example, stood a fine equestrian statue of the "enlightened despot" of the eighteenth century, Joseph II, the *beau idéal* of progressive-minded Viennese. Rising out of the Graben in the downtown area was a Trinity Column (*Pestsaeule*), a towering, white marble monument, replete with masses of billowing clouds, flitting cherubs, and grotesque religious symbolism. Kneeling is the Emperor Leopold I who was responsible for this baroque extravaganza. It was erected to express gratitude for the termination of a devastating epidemic in 1679. The best of Vienna's fountains was a creation in lead by Raphael Donner, situated in the *Neuer Markt* (New Market). At the center sat a chaste feminine representation of Providence, and on the rim four godlike figures symbolized important tributaries of the Danube.

Three mornings each week the larger city squares were transformed into hives of retail trade at wooden booths and temporary bazaars. Hundreds of peasant carts, after half a day's journey, perhaps, creaked into a square at two o'clock in the morning, and by six o'clock in the morning market transactions were over. At the spacious Am Hof, for example, the scene was one of aristocratic pageantry in the Middle Ages, vegetables and fruit in season, flowers, cheese, pots of cream and butter, game, and fuel were sold. At the Christmas season this square was given over to a fair for children; trees, special foods, toys, and dolls were offered for sale. Hucksters were frequently witty, and so too were eloquent women who chattered in the local dialect on all manner of topics sparing neither rulers, nor churchmen, nor people of quality; here, also, was the city arsenal stocked with thousands of tastefully arranged pieces of armor and trophies captured in war. In the nearby Judenplatz business establishments of wholesale merchants and textile warehouses were concentrated. The *Hoher Markt* (High Market), the oldest section of the town, was redolent with memories of imperial Rome; according to a plausible theory, the famous Stoic Emperor Marcus Aurelius died hereabouts in 180 A.D.

Although the most fashionable shops, the most elegant coffeehouses, and the principal hotels fronted on the *Kohlmarkt*, the Graben, or Kaerntnerstrasse, quality establishments were scattered promiscuously about the *Altstadt*. Shops were known by their painted signs and insignia, some of the devices truly artistic, not by the names of the proprietors. Tobacco articles could be purchased at "The Black Mother of God," and drugs at "the Holy Ghost." "To the Americans" read a colorful panel exhibiting an Indian chief in full ceremonial regalia. Illustrious contemporaries also figured on signs, one of young Queen Victoria over a millinery store displayed her physical charms to the maximum advantage. Striped poles designated barbershops, though Vienna barbers were much more than the word might suggest since, apart from tonsorial services, they performed minor surgery and dressed wounds. When shops were not open for business they were protected by

iron doors and shutters over glass windows. Itinerant peddlers hawked household provisions and dry goods along
the streets.

Through the community on the way to the Danube
Canal meandered the Vienna River, twenty yards across,
black and foul, noxious for citizens who did not take snuff
or smoke. When the volume of water was sufficient, the
stream supplied power for a few mills, though ordinarily
in the summer it was only a rivulet; in the winter snow
from the streets was dumped in.

Viennese houses were massive structures, as a rule, high
rise, ranging up to eight stories, and congested. At the
mid-nineteenth century there were approximately nine
thousand residential buildings, averaging about forty-two
inhabitants in each; like Paris, Vienna was overwhelmingly a city of apartment dwellers. Four hundred people
called the Trattner Hof on the Graben home, and five
times that many lived in the largest suburban block. Wine
cellars beneath some houses were as deep as the structures
above them were tall. Poorer families occupied the ground
level of residential buildings, the affluent the next two
floors, and middling income families the rest. Rooms
tended to be furnished simply—a porcelain stove, heavy
chairs, tables, and closets, uncarpeted parquet floors; between double windows, bolsters were lodged to keep out
the cold or to lean on and gawk at passers-by in clement
weather.

Water, which was chronically in short supply, had to be
fetched from public fountains or wells. Men and women
marched to fountains daily carrying on their backs a
wooden barrel (*butten*), flat on one side, and hauled their

burdens up as many flights of stairs as necessary. Teamsters with barrel-laden carts, drawn by horse or donkey, huckstered water from house to house or supplied regular customers. Houses that possessed wells commanded higher rentals.

Refuse and toilet sewage were removed by householders. As late as 1873, a British traveler wrote, "the drainage of the city is wretched and in certain parts the effluvia from the sewers et cetera is sickening." Candles and sputtering oil lamps supplied illumination in homes, shops, and mills. A neighborhood pattern of living prevailed, for a workman in a few minutes could walk to his job or to places purveying necessities and conveniences.

Because of the cramped, crowded quarters—dilapidated rotting slums in some cases—the Viennese spent a good deal of their leisure hours in coffeehouses or places of amusement or in parks and the encircling Vienna woods. Wealthy burghers escaped oppressive summer heat in comfortable suburban villas.

Omnibuses, driven by coachmen in blue coats and knee breeches and seating as many as ten passengers, furnished transportation from the big squares in the core of the city to improvised railway stations and to the suburbs, four miles or so away. Stagecoaches "nearly as capacious as steamboats" conveyed travelers to distant points not yet connected by rail. Hackney coaches of varied sizes and shapes were available for hire and also fiacres, one horse vehicles, capable of accommodating four. Moneyed families traveled about in handsome private carriages (likely enough built in Vienna); the equipages of aristocrats were normally preceded by a runner or two in livery, brandishing silver-headed sticks. Sleighs of the affluent resembled swans, griffins, dragons, or eagles, and were usually drawn by two horses and attended by outriders.

Since Viennese coachmen had a reputation for dexterity and for fast driving and since there were no sidewalks, pedestrians were ever alert. Loud and continuous "Ho hos!"—something between a shout and a scream—noisily reverberated through the canyon-like streets. The habit of piling logs on the street, to be sawed and split as fuel, men on horseback, and wheel-barrows, pushed not infrequently by women of Amazonian proportions, increased the hazards. "At every turn," declared an irritated foreigner, "you run the risk of being overturned by a carriage, a wagon or a wheelbarrow, the last being the most annoying of all the street nuisances of this city." Agile pedestrians saved themselves from injury by jumping on the steps of a passing carriage. To protect buildings along the busier arteries from the wheels of thundering vehicles, stout stone posts capped with iron were rooted in the ground. Quaint passageways beneath buildings (*Durchhaeuser*) permitted walkers to avoid street traffic or take short cuts to their destinations.

Placards on street corners advertised places of entertainment, folk festivals, and other pleasurable events. Since dancing was the supreme diversion of the Viennese, dance halls to satisfy all tastes and wallets were plentiful. Floors of oak were polished to the smoothness of a skating rink, and galleries and adjacent wings of halls were often reserved for eating and drinking. "Young ladies," reported a British observer, "sit like marketable articles awaiting the choice of a purchaser, and the men lounge about the doorways or stand about the buffet" until the sound of music gave the signal to seize a partner.

The subterranean Elyseum ballroom, which could accommodate hundreds of couples, was decorated to resemble the quarters of the globe. Even larger were the Apollo Saal, in which ten thousand frantic revelers could waltz or execute a gallopade, and the Odeon, noted for its gorgeously frescoed ceiling and glass doors opening onto a garden, where the orchestra was installed in a small temple. More exotic still was the Sperl, located like the Odeon in the Leopoldstadt; it was divided into four compartments, each representing a continent and each having its own band.

Beer saloons and wine cellars enjoyed a generous patronage. If the weather was good, ordinary Viennese congregated in suburban garden taverns or their little courtyards to drink new wine (*heuriger*), chaffer, listen to violin or zither music, and sing folk melodies.

> *Wer nicht liebt Wein, Weib, Gesang,*
> *Bleibt ein Narr sein Leben lang.*

"Who likes not wine, woman, and song, Remains a fool his whole life long." ran a familiar *heuriger* ditty. A bush or branch of fir stuck on a pole over the entrance to a wine resort indicated that a new vintage was available inside. Bringing their own food, merrymakers sat on wooden benches at long tables.

About eighty coffeehouses, a specialty of Vienna, were frequented by men, though some set aside quarters for ladies. Except for a few luxury establishments in the inner city, coffeehouses were primitive and dimly lighted, and rooms were likely to be filled with smoke. Patrons lingered for hours on end sipping coffee (or tea or chocolate), smoking, reading newspapers, playing billiards, chess or cards, exchanging opinions on literature and music, politics and economics, or sealing business transactions. A guest could have letters or messages addressed to him at his customary coffeehouse. Some Viennese took their seats at the same table almost daily from youth to old age; knowing waiters served personal mixtures of coffee and placed the favorite newspapers at the elbow of regular patrons.

The Vienna of 1848 boasted five playhouses of general significance. The Carinthian Gate theater (*Kaerntnerthor*) presented opera and ballet almost exclusively and boasted an orchestra of sixty musicians, reputed to be the best in Europe. Nestling in a niche of the rambling Hofburg was the century-old Burgtheater, offering tragedies and comedies. In 1862, the American minister at the Hapsburg court, John L. Motley, described the Burgtheater as "the funniest, shabbiest, most ramshackle old place that you can imagine. The chandelier will hardly give sufficient light for an ordinary saloon. You can hardly see across the house, although it is very narrow and as straight as an omnibus." This theater was the preferred playhouse of the court and elegant society, and star performers were rewarded with state decorations and pensions.

Outside the city walls, the *Theater an der Wien* was not only the most spacious playhouse of Vienna, but was unsurpassed on the Continent. Notable premières once staged there included Mozart's *Magic Flute* and Beethoven's *Fidelio*. On another level, the Leopoldstadt theater catered to popular tastes, presenting humorous and satirical farces, full of allusions to local manners and foibles which were frequently offbeat. Since the Viennese vernacular was commonly spoken, patrons from abroad had extreme difficulty in following the dialogue. Mirth, song, and perpetual laughter also reigned supreme in the Josephstadt theater. Curtains at playhouses rose at seven in the evening.

For outdoor recreation skaters used the Danube or the highly favored Vienna river in the winter, and for the rest of the year there were excursions to the delightful Vienna woods or to a public park. In no other European city could inhabitants get so quickly into wide open spaces. The huge Prater, a two thousand acre tract encircled by the Danube, furnished unadulterated fun for young and old, for the smart set, and for ordinary folk. On fine days, the first of May especially, fashionable equipages and festively cos-tumed horsemen thronged the principal thoroughfare (*Hauptallee*), cut through forests and lined with a double row of horse-chestnut trees; side paths were restricted to pedestrians. In the annual May Day parade, the handsome coach of the emperor might be seen, pulled by six white horses, with two servants occupying a rumble seat at the rear; carriages of pillars of society might be accompanied by as many as a dozen uniformed footmen and guards.

Herds of deer blithely roamed one section of the Prater and at the southern end an oval (*Freudenau*) for horse racing was laid out. Popular excitement over racing reached a peak toward the end of May when a dangerous, thrilling steeplechase was held. The course traversed four miles of hunting ground, studded with more than a score of obstacles, two brooks among them, and a wall of earth facing a treacherous swamp. From a wharf on the edge of the Prater, steamers, "painted, gilded, velvet-furnished and mirrored," departed for journeys on the Danube.

The area known as the "Peoples' Prater" (*Wurstel*

Prater) offered mass entertainment on the scale of a gigantic fair. Mountebanks and jugglers, magicians and rope dancers, acrobats and exotic animals, stage shows and dance bands, cafés and bowling greens competed for customers at this "paradise of the Viennese." Bands playing different tunes, the shrills cries of showmen and peddlers, boisterous laughing and talking created a veritable bedlam; intoxication was a rarity though, and there was little quarreling, even with practical jokesters. Picnic areas were plentiful and knots of listeners clustered round amateur musicians in meadows. Several times a year mammoth displays of fireworks were set off, ending in a deafening explosion. At nine o'clock in the evening the great bell on St. Stephen's warned merrymakers to start home lest they find the portals of the inner city closed. When Goethe's Mephistopheles wished to praise the diversions of the witches' Sabbath he said, "Here it is as jolly as in the Prater."

More sedate than the Prater, and less animated, was the far smaller Augarten, frequented by the well to do in search of relaxation. French-styled formal gardens surrounded a large palace and a famous Augarten porcelain factory in the park. Annually in July, a gay festival with diversified amusements, from swings to a miniature railway, and leather-lunged hawkers attracted throngs to a pleasure ground on the meadow of St. Bridget (*Brigittenau*). And the *Volksgarten*, or "People's Garden," close by the imperial palace, was another popular resort. It was not unusual for a thousand couples to waltz in the pavilion of the park, while a multitude looked on or listened to a band concert. By night flickering lights converted lovely flower beds, shrubs, and trees into a veritable fairyland; now and then the gaiety ceased with a brilliant pyrotechnic display. A Doric temple in the garden enclosed a chaste sculpture done by Canova, "Theseus Conquering the Centaur," imitative of a monument in Athens.

Such were the cultural, educational, and recreational facilities of Vienna, such the makeup of the capital city when young Franz Josef assumed sovereign authority.

⋞ 2 ⋟

Transformation of a Metropolis

At THE mid-nineteenth century, Vienna ranked second in size only to London and Paris among European cities. Machine industrialization in the three preceding decades and the advent of the steamboat, railways, and telegraph facilitated the expansion of trade and commerce. And Vienna evolved, it must be emphasized, as the capital of the Hapsburg realm of many tongues, almost as big as Texas. It was the seat of the imperial court and focal point of the disparate nobility of the empire, of a very large bureaucracy, and of the fighting services.

> *There where the Danube broadly sweeps,*
> *'Mid islands willow grown,*
> *The City of St. Stephen stands,*
> *An Empire's lovely throne.*

That "lovely throne," which seemed to be as firm as the Great Pyramid itself, was shaken to its foundations during political convulsions of 1848. Low standards of living among the industrial working class and the aspirations of the intelligentsia for freedom and popular government, combined with restlessness among the leaders of the non-German nationalities of the Monarchy, produced a succession of revolutionary upheavals. Vienna in particular reverberated to a February rising in Paris, which led to the establishment of a republican system. On March 13, insurgent elements, headed by students, forced the detested Metternich to resign, soon secured abolition of the hated censorship, and extracted promises of a constitutional regime.

By autumn, however, disunity among the revolutionaries and the unswerving loyalty of the Hapsburg armies ruined the great expectations of the Viennese rebels. Similarly, Czech and Italian national insurgencies had been beaten down, but the Hungarians were not subdued until the summer of 1849. Some 2,400 Viennese citizens were haled before drumhead courts. Though only about one-fifth were punished, more than a score suffered the death penalty. Admirers of the revolutionaries regarded them as martyrs to the cause of human freedom and dignity, and almost annually thereafter demonstrated in their honor.

During the revolutionary storms, the Viennese were awakened to a sense of political awareness, never thereafter lost. And a small segment of the adult males was given nominal control over city administration through a municipal council. This body of 120 was elected by three classes of male citizens, divided mainly on the basis of direct taxes that they paid.

After the defeat of Austria in 1859 in war with France and Italian Sardinia, the Danubian metropolis was at last accorded real autonomy. A strong majority of Liberals was elected to the city council, and their ascendancy lasted nearly two generations. The economy of the community quickly recovered from the disruptive consequences of the revolution of 1848; new banks such as the famous Credit

Anstalt (1855) of the House of Rothschild were founded, and many other business enterprises were started on their careers.

Agents of the crown missed no opportunity to burnish the Vienna image of Franz Josef as a benevolent father. Popular enthusiasm for the dynasty touched a high point in 1854 when the Emperor married his cousin, Princess Elizabeth of Bavaria, a tall, slender, radiant girl of only sixteen, who became the loveliest empress of her time. News of the birth of a son, the Crown Prince Rudolph, in 1858, elicited general rejoicing; his three sisters, one older than he, were welcomed by Vienna with only less fervor.

Before the postrevolutionary decade had run its course, traditional Viennese folk customs and habits of living had been revived. For the young in years or in spirit, the carnival season (*Fasching*) meant frolic and fun, feasting and finery. Some forty days a year were set apart as holidays, celebrating the birthday of the Emperor or marking a religious fete. Religious solemnities reached their apogee during Holy Week; on Maundy Thursday, Emperor and Empress piously observed an elaborate ritual of feeding twelve old and poor men and women and washing their feet. If the weather was fair on Corpus Christi Day, Franz Josef and the imperial household took part in a colorful religious procession in the inner city.

Foreigner after foreigner visiting Vienna remarked upon the native addiction to the pleasures of the table and the food and wine specialities of the community. Commentators from abroad frequently associated cuisine delights with the proverbial Viennese *Gemütlichkeit,* a term defying precise translation but suggesting geniality, good humor, cordiality, and kindliness.

As a kind of Christmas gift in 1857, the Emperor announced plans to tear down the ancient fortifications of the capital and to merge the inner city with its fringing suburbs. Work got underway promptly. The central feature of the reconstruction and beautification was a majestic boulevard—or rather a series of eight interlinked boulevards—the Ringstrasse, sixty yards wide and over two and one half miles long, which encircled most of the inner city; a quay beside the Danube Canal covered the final portion. As token concessions to history, small fragments of the medieval battlements were left intact. Trees lined the noble thoroughfare, and gas blazing from triple burners furnished illumination. The official opening of the Ringstrasse, dazzling symbol of the "new Vienna," took place in 1865.

Almost three-fifths of the land of the former glacis and land made available by the demolition of the walls were allocated to parks, gardens, and streets. The remainder was divided about equally between sites for public buildings and parcels, which meant that more than two hundred acres were disposed of to private interests. Funds that accrued from the sale were applied to defraying the costs of reconstruction, laying out streets and parks, and—most important—erecting public buildings.

Along or near the Ring, governmental and cultural structures, palaces, and commercial buildings were raised in a variety of architectural styles. In the first wave of construction, edifices for the cultural arts, crowned by a huge opera house, were built. Next, between 1877 and 1891, a *Bourse* (Stock Exchange), the *Votivkirche*, law courts, a city hall, a home for the Austrian imperial parliament, a new university, a new court theater, and museums of fine arts and natural history were dedicated in rapid succession. The ancient Hofburg was enlarged, and an imposing, ornate gateway facing the inner city took the place of the old Burgtheater. Pleasant open spaces were laid out along the Ring, as, for instance, the *Stadt Park* (City Park), the first large municipal playground of Vienna.

Take it all in all, the Ringstrasse itself, the stately edifices, the fine parks and statuary in stone and metal formed one of the grand urban sights of Europe, which Viennese proudly hailed as the *via triumphalis.* So greatly impressed was a lad from an Austrian village that he would one day write, "The entire Ringstrasse affected me like a fairy tale out of the *Arabian Nights.*" His name was Adolf Hitler.

Urban development in Vienna did not stop, however, with the creation of the Ringstrasse and its architectural glories—which will be described later. New and fine stores, new factories, and banking houses were erected. Many joint-stock companies were chartered by the government, and a veritable mania gripped the highly speculative construction industry. Building firms grew like mushrooms, bidding up the prices of residential blocks and plots of ground; partly in anticipation of a world exhibition planned for 1873, many cafés, restaurants, and elegant hotels were rushed to completion. Stocks of all sorts of firms flooded the exchange, some of them utterly worthless, yet the prices soared to fantastic heights.

Periodically, in the late 1860's and early 1870's, prices on the stock exchange broke sharply. The grand climax started on May 9, 1873—Black Friday—when big quantities of securities were thrown on the market, causing prices to crack and canceling paper winnings. Even blue-chip stocks declined from 30 to 50 per cent in value. With a resounding crash, the artificial prosperity collapsed, ruining thousands of households and leading several insolvent speculators to take their own lives. Confusion in the business community was reflected in unemployment and widespread worker distress. Well-managed banks and the Austrian government intervened, it is true, to restore a measure of stability, but the crippled economy of Vienna stagnated for the rest of 1870's.

A matter of days before the terrible panic began, the great International Exhibition opened. An area of four hundred acres in the Prater was crowded with buildings in which exhibits were displayed; the biggest of them, a huge rotunda reminiscent of the Pantheon in Rome, was the largest roofed structure in the world. Fair grounds were artistically laid out and a bewildering variety of facilities for eating, drinking, and entertainment was available.

All the world sent products to the fair; there were some forty thousand exhibitors showing their wares, and juries awarded twenty thousand medals. "No pencil will ever succeed in depicting its beauties," wrote the American Professor James M. Hart of the Exhibition, "no tongue will ever give more than a faint echo of its wonders." He likened a morning's stroll through the fair grounds to a tour of the world—Japanese idols, American artificial teeth, Russian sables, Krupp's grim cannon, Bohemian glass. "The teachings of art and science at Vienna were a curriculum transcending that of a college or university," Hart thought.

European royalties and celebrities congregated in Vienna to an extent unapproached since the Congress of Vienna in 1815. The prince of Wales, the Russian czar, the German emperor and his diplomatic virtuoso, Otto von Bismarck, the Italian king, and lesser crowned heads mingled with some seven million commoners at the Exhibition. The colossal rotunda remained a permanent reminder of what was intended to be one of Vienna's finest hours—and indeed was in some respects.

For three decades, starting in 1861, the municipal government of Vienna was dominated by the Liberal Party, heir of the moderate liberalism of 1848, but wedded to the ideas of restricting suffrage to the well-to-do few and of minimum intervention by government in the economic sphere. City councilmen continued to be chosen on the inequitable three class (*curia*) system. Seldom did as many as half of the electors appear at the polls, and on occasion the proportion dropped as low as 10 per cent. In 1861, only about eighteen thousand citizens were enfranchised, but in 1885, following prolonged agitation, the voting right was extended to men who paid as little as five gulden (roughly two dollars) in direct taxes. That reform tripled the electorate, yet at least three out of four of the adult males of Vienna were still ineligible to vote. Councilmen had to be voters at least thirty years of age, and the mayor, the key personality in municipal government, was chosen by the council from its membership; before the mayor could take office he had to be confirmed by the emperor.

Liberal administrations, in addition to sharing in the Ringstrasse enterprise, accomplished many worthwhile improvements. Chronic deficiencies in the supply of water, for example, were temporarily overcome by bringing water of excellent quality across aqueducts and through mountain tunnels from an Alpine region, fifty-six miles away. So large, however, was the increase in water consumption that the suburbs soon experienced shortages, necessitating rationing and reliance on fountains as previously.

Aided by the imperial and the provincial treasuries, the Vienna municipality carried out a long needed regulation of the Danube. Almost every year, floods had driven families in the Danube Canal zone from their homes, destroying household furnishings and ruining goods in warehouses. The gigantic task of digging a straight, eight-mile bed for the Canal was practically completed in five years, the first ship passing through in 1875.

The Liberals also pointed with pride to the construction of new hospitals and other health facilities and to more efficient police and fire protection. Due to the scarcity of space in existing graveyards, the municipal government purchased a huge tract of land, subsequently added to, for the Central Cemetery, five miles out from the center of the city. Sections were allocated to the several religious faiths, and burials in older cemeteries were prohibited; in 1881, the remains of Viennese cultural workers of high distinction were reinterred in a special area of the Central Cemetery.

Modes of transportation in the Hapsburg metropolis passed through several stages. Horse cars first appeared in 1865, and traffic grew rapidly—twelve and one half million passengers being moved five years later. Cars were coupled in strings of three, each small and one usually reserved for smokers. They were reputedly dirty and slow, for horses merely jogged along, loud-sounding bells around their necks—" . . . snails on wheels," remarked a disgruntled foreigner. Special cars transported wage earners going to and from work and school children at cheap rates.

Steam and electricity were introduced in the 1880's to drive streetcars, and in that decade bicycles attained such popularity that legislation had to be enacted to regulate their use. Initially, bicycle riding was only a sport with cyclists engaging in contests of speed or endurance; then workers rode bicycles to their jobs or on jaunts into the countryside, and bolder members of the gentler sex followed suit. Year by year, electricity gradually replaced gas for street lighting, first in the metropolitan core (1882), later in the suburbs, and simultaneously the earliest telephones were installed, seven hundred being in service in 1885. Owning to its basically laissez-faire philosophy and fiscal conservatism, the Liberal council did nothing substantial to improve housing for the proletariat, who lived in congested, unsanitary slums.

As was true of other metropolises of the nineteenth century, Vienna exerted a magnetic attraction upon men and women born outside its borders who desired better material and cultural opportunities. Whereas at 1800 about 90 per cent of the population were Viennese in origin, the proportion in the Greater Vienna of 1891 had fallen to approximately 35 per cent. Possibly 55 per cent had moved in from countries comprising the Austrian Empire other than from Hungary and Bosnia which accounted for another 8 per cent, leaving about 2 per cent of foreign birth.

Newcomers who had emigrated from the northern provinces, Sudeten Germans and Czechs, probably comprised nearly one-half the people in the Greater Vienna of 1891. German in speech, the Sudetens readily became assimilated with the older residents; at one point, one-third of the memorials to scholars in the University arcades honored Sudeten Germans. Whereas the Czech minority equalled about 2 per cent of the Viennese population in 1850, it had risen to 5 per cent by 1890 and would go beyond that level. Like the Czechs, small colonies of Poles, Ukrainians, and southern Slavs, contingents of the Magyars, Italians, and Greeks set up benevolent, cultural, and athletic societies. At 1873, two Vienna newspapers were being printed in the Czech and Magyar languages, and one each in Polish, Ukrainian, Croatian, and Hebrew.

From the East, immigrants of the Jewish tradition wandered to Vienna in large numbers. By 1880, Jewish residents exceeded seventy thousand, ten times more than thirty years earlier, and comprised nearly 10 per cent of the total population, a ratio that persisted thereafter. Before the mid-nineteenth century a small, though important, community of Jews lived in Vienna. Best known was the Rothschild family, powerful in the financial affairs of the city and of the Hapsburg Monarchy as a whole. Fabulously rich, patrons of culture, and generous in philanthropy, the Rothschilds were well assimilated in the Viennese environment, as was usually the case with other established Jewish households. A wide chasm yawned between assimilated Jewry and its immigrant coreligionists from the East.

Apparently, it was in 1882 that the first organization in Vienna to wage a regular campaign against Jewry came into existence. Since Jews were closely identified with the Liberals, agitators hostile to Jewry leveled attacks on their party, and denunciations became more vehement after the enfranchisement of the "five gulden" men. Anti-Jewish councilmen repeatedly converted the municipal legislature into a veritable bear garden. In 1885 a destructive riot erupted in suburban Leopoldstadt, which resembled the ghetto quarter of an east European town, and howling mobs damaged Jewish property, yelling savagely, "Down with the Jews," "Down with the Blood-Suckers." Since the police proved powerless to stop the disorders, which spread to other wards, army contingents had to be sent in to restore peace; many rioters were injured and more were thrown into jail.

As of 1888, Vienna had upwards of 7,500 large-scaled and middle-sized industrial, commercial, and banking enterprises and over 46,000 small plants and businesses. While some of the workmen belonged to the "labor aristocracy," the majority owned little or no property beyond personal belongings, and thus may accurately be described as proletarian. It is this class particularly that will be considered in the section that follows.

Into the 1880's, at any rate, a working week of seventy hours, Sundays and holidays included, was not unusual, and the work week was longer in little shops than in big mills; in summer months workers in breweries often put in eighteen hours at a stretch. Women made up a high percentage of the work force in factories and on construction jobs, as well as in the domestic services; husband and wife working teams were quite common. Many women could obtain only seasonal employment, and attractive girls learned that the chances of obtaining or holding a job improved if they yielded to the importunities of overseers and foremen. Exploitation of children and of apprentices, who often served three years merely for their food and possibly lodgings, was widespread.

Wages of proletarians provided for little beyond basic food and clothing necessities, cramped apartments, and cheap recreation. On a working day, breakfast consisted of coffee and a roll, followed by a midmorning snack of bread and butter; the noonday meal was one of soup, vegetables, and bread, followed by possibly beer or coffee and bread in the middle of the afternoon and again in the evening. Working class budgets permitted an occasional sausage dish and a piece of beef or horsemeat or fish on Sundays and holidays.

For many proletarian families housing, shabby, congested, poorly lighted, and innocent of plumbing facilities, left much, very much, to be desired. The demand for flats pushed rentals upward until they absorbed about a quarter of the income of a typical working class household. It was disclosed in a sensational investigation (1894) by the distinguished University economist, Eugene von Philippovich, that occupants per room in Vienna were nearly twice as numerous as in Paris, itself no paradise for ordinary workers. The utmost squalor, he revealed, prevailed in dark, damp, cellar slums, scarcely fit for animals; children ran about stark naked.

In barrack-like quarters, four or more families crowded into a single room. In instances, thirty or more persons of both sexes occupied one room, some of them sleeping on the floor; in smaller mills, workers sometimes slept in their place of employment. An American who studied conditions among women employed as common laborers concluded: "The meanest animal in the royal stables is better cared for than those women." In many proletarian tenements, toilets and water faucets were located in hallways and might serve a hundred or more people; baths were taken in municipal bathing establishments.

It must be said, however, that many immigrant families had known only squalid, overcrowded, housing conditions in the communities that they had left to move to Vienna, and that the situation was probably worse in Budapest and Moscow, for example. Be that as it may, congestion contributed to a high rate of illegitimacy and mortality. Although the Viennese death rate dropped sharply in the course of the nineteenth century, the incidence of death ran higher in proletarian districts than in the more favored inner city; for many an underprivileged resident of the industrial wards, life was "nasty, brutish, and short."

Among other things, the unhealthy social environment encouraged prostitution; factory girls and waitresses varied their long, dull hours of employment and pieced out low wages through illicit, business-like romance. Prostitution and therewith venereal disease were standing and intensifying Viennese problems. Following an investigation, in which eminent University professors of medicine took part, a statute of 1873 legalized professional prostitution; girls had to be at least fourteen years old (the age was subsequently raised), to carry a health book (later a card) indicating their physical condition, and to undergo periodic medical examinations.

Enterprising proletarians, implemented projects to advance—or at least to protect—living standards. To cut food costs, for instance, a group of Vienna weavers and apprentices banded together (1864) in a consumers' co-operative, patterned on an English model; it was designed to eliminate the profits of shopkeepers. Although dealt a temporary setback by the business recession that began in 1873, the co-operative idea took firm root, and before long loans at low rates of interest were made available to members of co-operatives, and plants were built to process foodstuffs and to manufacture household necessities.

It was permissible under Austrian law to organize wageworkers for social and educational purposes, but not to form unions for collective bargaining. Nor could mass meetings be held in the open without explicit police authorization. Nevertheless, toward the end of 1869 some fifteen thousand workmen assembled peacefully on the Ringstrasse in support of a petition to the Austrian parliament asking for the right to organize unions, to conduct strikes, to have unfettered freedom of assembly and press, and to acquire the privilege of voting. Accused of plotting revolution—the uprisings of 1848 were still green in memory—the leaders of the mass rally were seized by the police, and several were convicted of treason, though soon set free. The Austrian government in 1870, however, legalized trade union activity, though under close police surveillance; physical violence in connection with strikes would be severely punished.

Police watched foreigners in Vienna with great vigilance, and suspicious characters were expelled with scant ceremony. Yet street convulsions in 1882 were the worst Vienna had known since 1848; riotous proletarians went berserk, and troops that were called in dispersed angry crowds at the point of the bayonet. When outbreaks recurred in 1884, martial law was imposed, which rendered easier the suppression of societies suspected of adherence to anarchism and the punishment of the leaders. Partisans of Marxian Socialism presently published (1886) a newspaper, *Die Gleichheit* (Equality), which summoned anticapitalist forces to consolidate—an appeal that speedily yielded results.

The Austrian parliament in the 1880's adopted legislation intended to alleviate the worst evils of wage earners. Managers were ordered, for example, to install safety devices and to keep workshops clean, adequately ventilated, and lighted. An act of 1883 created an embryonic factory inspection system, but the inspectors, few in number, lacked sufficient authority to compel improvements in working conditions, and in any case the law applied only to the larger plants. Other measures prohibited employment of young children, restricted hours of work for teenagers and women, fixed the maximum workday for nearly all employees at eleven hours with at least one hour of rest, and prescribed that workers were to be free on Sunday or another day each week.

Yet loopholes in the legislation, evasions, and a special concession to Viennese newspapers which wanted early Monday morning editions, somewhat nullified the intended benefits. As in Bismarckian Germany, Austrian enactments (1887) set up programs of compulsory accident and sickness insurance for the employed. These innovations, elementary and circumscribed though they were, started Vienna along the road to becoming a "welfare city."

Protracted debate over the integration of the suburbs beyond the outer walls, or *Linienwall*, with the rest of Vienna culminated in 1890 in their annexation. The old defenses were removed, and on their site a wide concentric street (*Guertel*) was constructed, on which railways were laid, tying in with the general pattern of Vienna transport. Although hated imposts were no longer collected on goods passing from the outer suburbs into the metropolitan area, tolls had to be paid at the approaches to the enlarged city.

The merger more than tripled the size of the municipality, and the population, which had grown from about 500,000 to beyond 800,000, exceeded 1,365,000 in the

Greater Vienna. To the existing ten wards, nine more were added; the new districts of Ottakring and Hernals were overwhelmingly proletarian in makeup with factories, workshops, and slum sections, while Doebling and Grinzing preserved their quaint village character.

Concurrently with territorial enlargement, a new institution to administer the municipality was created. Called the *Stadtrat*, or "inner committee," its members were chosen by the council from its own ranks. This body, which met frequently, was charged with the appointment of city officials and exercised general supervision over municipal business. By 1890 the Liberal Party, riven by intense factionalism and its public image tarnished by corruption on the part of some of its councilmen, had declined sharply in prestige. Competing mass parties, the Christian Socialists and the Social Democrats, pushed hard to gain control of the government. After the seating toward the end of the 1880's of a few councilmen later known as Christian Socialists, sessions, which hitherto had been placid and rather academic, became explosive and demagogic.

3

The Kingdom of Learning

EXPANSION of educational institutions and the spread of literacy were distinctive hallmarks of Western society in the second half of the nineteenth century, and Vienna participated richly in these gains. In the revolutionary year of 1848, an Austrian ministry of education was set up, which engaged a progressively minded professor of philosophy at Prague University, Franz S. Exner, as technical specialist on school reform. Up to a point, he commanded the support of Count Leo Thun-Hohenstein, a Bohemian aristocrat of conservative outlook, who served for more than a decade as minister of education.

If the higher goals of the reformers were thwarted by the influences of the Roman Catholic Church, at least modest improvements were effected in the elementary schools (*Volkschulen*). And at the end of the 1860's, Austrian legislation practically eliminated the role of churchmen in education, required children to attend common schools for at least six years, and introduced new subjects into the curriculum. Teacher training institutes were organized and salaries were raised, making it no longer necessary for a teacher to piece out his income by employment as choirmaster or custodian in a church. Women were

46

increasingly engaged to teach girls, who were strictly segregated from boys in Vienna schools.

Although the ratio of teachers who taught nearly doubled between 1870 and 1890, congested classrooms were a standing grievance of all concerned. Whereas in 1860, 30,000 Viennese pupils were studying in elementary schools, attendance thirty years later had jumped to almost 87,000, and in 1903 approached 200,000. It was estimated that in 1890 over 85 per cent of the Viennese were literate in contrast to about 60 per cent at the mid-century.

Publicly financed secondary schools were added to the traditional classical *gymnasia*, conducted mostly by Roman Catholic religious orders. All told, seventeen institutions were offering this type of secondary education by 1900. Newer secondary schools, *realschulen*, preparing youths for technological and commercial colleges, never attained the prestige of the *gymnasia*, but both were attended largely by children of well-to-do homes. *Gymnasia* enrollment nearly doubled between 1860 and 1890, and pupils in other secondary schools exceeded 20,000 in 1890, a fivefold growth in thirty years; about 9,000 more children attended church affiliated schools.

Progress was registered in other Viennese facilities for culture and learning—continuation classes for apprentices, centers for adult education, and lending libraries, generally under Roman Catholic auspices. Growth of the literate public and rising interest in current affairs prompted the multiplication of Vienna newspapers. Unexampled press freedom in 1848 encouraged a flood of new papers, mostly small and short-lived. Thereafter, the government instituted extensive controls over publications, but enforcement fluctuated being most rigorous when a grave domestic or international crisis arose. Before a paper was started, the proprietor had to obtain official sanction. Censors read each issue of a paper, striking out anything regarded as subversive or dangerous; an entire issue sometimes was banned and the responsible editor imprisoned.

Due to the rigors and vagaries of the censorship, Viennese journalists learned to write cautiously, and alert readers habitually searched between the lines for meanings. It was unlawful to hawk papers on the streets; they could only be obtained through the mails or purchased at licensed tobacco shops. In any case, a fee had to be paid for each copy of a newspaper (indicated by a black seal resembling a postage stamp). Leading liberal papers incessantly clamored for broader freedom of press, though their linkage with financial syndicates sometimes exerted an inhibiting influence on what was printed.

Of the papers that survived the authoritarian regime after the 1848 revolution, the *Presse,* in spite of a reputation for venality, probably commanded the most influence outside of official circles. In pithy editorials, it proclaimed liberal principles under the slogan "Equal rights for all"; sales approached fifteen thousand, a figure previously unheard of in Viennese journalism. The *Presse* fell on hard times when leading staff members resigned and established the *Neue Freie Presse* (1864), which developed into the foremost Vienna daily, and one of the most highly esteemed newspapers of the world. Its proprietors avoided sensationalism and insisted on sober treatment of current happenings. So great did the influence of the paper become under the industrious and domineering proprietor, Moritz

Benedict, that it was said jestingly that next to him Franz Josef was the most important personality in Austria.

The *Neue Freie Presse* upheld the tenets of liberalism espoused by the Liberal party and was distinctly the mouthpiece of big financial and industrial interests. For information on world affairs it leaned heavily on English and French news services, and when interpreting international events, it tended strongly to diffuse opinions favored by the foreign office. "The greater part of what does duty for Austrian opinion," thought an informed but shrewish British publicist, "is dictated or suggested to the public by the editor-proprietor of the *Neue Freie Presse*."

The paper prided itself on authoritative economic articles and superior literary style, particularly in *feuilletons*, brief essays on serious matters, or travelogues, or short stories, or bright, witty pieces of froth. The size of the daily soon grew to thirty pages, with a Sunday edition of eighty pages; by 1890, about forty thousand copies were being printed.

Second in bourgeois respectability, though ultimately an easy first in circulation, was the *Neues Wiener Tageblatt* (1867), edited by the talented Moritz Szeps. It, too, was a staunch partisan of civil rights, engaged writers of quality, and devoted a good deal of space to economic and social reports. For official announcements, the Austrian government used the *Wiener Zeitung*, oldest of Vienna's papers, started in 1703, and the foreign office disseminated news and views in the columns of the *Fremdenblatt*.

Viewpoints of Catholic conservatism were set forth in the *Wienerkirchenzeitung*, which endeavored not only to counteract liberal journalism, but to invigorate the spirit of Catholicism. Its partner, the small *Vaterland* (1859), had only a limited subscription list, but as an unsleeping adversary of liberalism it carried weight in clerical and conservative quarters. Weekly or monthly papers that championed the interests of the proletariat frequently had trouble with the censors and invariably ceased publication in a short while.

Informal education through the press and formal schooling molded the popular culture in Vienna. On a higher level, at the University of Vienna, "the most beautiful and valuable jewel of the Austrian crown," the faculties of philosophy (embracing the humanities, the natural sciences, and mathematics), medicine, law (which included political science and economics), and Roman Catholic theology cultivated mature learning and research. Comprehensive reforms, sponsored by Minister of Education Thun, inaugurated a new era of University prosperity. Greater freedom for teachers and students, the seminar method of instruction, and a wider selection of subjects were introduced. Costs of maintenance, faculty salaries included, were borne by the Austrian government, and student fees were minimal.

Agitation for secularization of the University of Vienna in liberal, professorial, and student circles was lively, persistent, and in time successful. To illustrate, on the occasion of the five hundredth anniversary of the establishment of the University, (1865) a large majority of the professors petitioned the minister of education to eliminate the influence of the Roman Church, and when the plea was rejected, many of the signers held aloof from the commemorative festivities. Students on their part kicked up a rumpus when the authorities announced that the celebration would be held in August instead of on March 12, the traditionally accepted date of the beginning of the University's existence. But on March 12, 1848, the revolutionary wave had commenced to roll, and the official world, dreading lest that day might set off unwelcome student disturbances, insisted on August. Street demonstrations, in which liberal students were arrayed against clerically minded mates, ensued, and the former group celebrated the March 12 anniversary with a nightlong commemoration of their own.

It was extremely annoying to liberal spirits to hear the rector of the time, the distinguished anatomist Joseph Hyrtl, a devout Catholic, extol the superiority of religion over science in a jubilee address. But tempers were mollified when an honorary doctorate was conferred upon John Stuart Mill, foremost English philosopher of the liberal faith. Pan-German overtones marked the anniversary festivities, one speaker saying, "Let it be the task of German [language] universities to train men fitted for a future German national parliament." University student societies displayed strong Pan-German and anti-Jewish feelings.

At 1860 the University of Vienna enrolled approximately 3,000 learners and thirty years later about 6,200, much the largest proportion in medicine, the faculties of law and philosophy coming next, and theology trailing far behind. With many reservations, women in 1878 were grudgingly admitted to study in the philosophical faculty, though few actually matriculated. Ranking below the University in the kingdom of learning were the Technological College (or Polytechnic), whose student personnel increased from 1,200 in the early 1850's to over 2,200 in 1900, and centers for advanced instruction in music, the fine arts, Oriental languages, commerce, earth culture, and veterinary medicine.

Scholarly societies and institutes in Vienna reinforced what was being done at the highest institutions of learning. Of them the Austrian Academy of Sciences, dating from 1847, had by far the largest importance; election to this body was the loftiest honor to which a Viennese intellectual could aspire. The Academy presented lectures, published learned literature, financed scientific enterprises, and in general promoted the advancement of learning. More or less on the model of the Academy, the free professions and divisions of medicine and science formed learned societies that brought out scholarly journals, proceedings, and books; some of them owned extensive research libraries.

The renown of Vienna in medical science, built up during the years, persisted into the twentieth century. Eminent professors established pathological anatomy and physical diagnosis as the guidelines in the art of healing the globe around. The vast General Hospital with its maze of wards and clinics, spoken of as "the cathedral of European medicine," provided exceptional opportunities for the study of every kind of disease and an inexhaustible supply of material for clinical instruction and observation. Since virtually everyone who died in this hospital was given an autopsy, plenty of cadavers were available for the instruction of students. Certain medical specialties were carried forward in the splendid military medical school and hospital, the Josephinum.

Karl von Rokitansky, the foremost Viennese medical professor at the mid-century, pioneered in teaching pathological anatomy as an independent discipline. He classified types of diseases with their causes and symptoms on an anatomical basis. His massive *Manual of Pathologic Anatomy* served generations of students, though it incorporated some curious and false hypotheses, which Rokitansky reluctantly renounced when they were exploded; in turn, he upset many accepted theories on the basis of observations in autopsies. He avoided living patients, but performed in excess of seventy thousand autopsies and prepared vivid, accurate reports on many of them. Younger colleagues were inspired by him to seek clarity in understanding and expression. "Rokitansky taught us to think anatomically at the bedside," declared one disciple, "and at the autopsy table to weave the individual phases of the morbid process into the pattern of clinical progress."

Much influenced by experimentalists in Paris and Bohemian-born like Rokitansky, Joseph Skoda excelled in anatomical diagnosis and took little interest in therapy. As shown in his famous book *Percussion and Auscultation*, which passed through many editions, he was concerned primarily with diseases of the heart and chest. Despite a reputation for roughness in handling patients (a common criticism of Vienna professors), Skoda was sought out by the ill of the highest classes of society and consulted by ailing affluent foreigners. His most talented student, Ferdinand von Hebra, created the science of skin diseases, which hitherto had been the happy hunting ground of charlatans, and made Vienna a Mecca for dermatologists. A skillful diagnostician, Hebra perfected clinical techniques taught by Skoda and classified diseases of the skin on the basis of pathological anatomy. He consolidated his international fame with a book, *On Diseases of the Skin*, lucid and vivid in composition, and as editor of a journal for skin specialists.

Hebra befriended Ignaz P. Semmelweis, a noble and tragic figure in Vienna medical annals. Appalled by the high mortality rate among women because of puerperal fever at the time of childbirth, Semmelweis came to the conclusion that the disease was due to septic infection. He required students working with maternity cases to apply a disinfectant to their hands, with the result that deaths dropped sharply. Praised by some of his contemporaries, but ridiculed by other professional men of standing, he lacked literary talent to defend himself in convincing fashion. A Hungarian by birth, Semmelweis accepted appointment to a professorship in Budapest University, but, his mind became unhinged, and he returned to Vienna for treatment, where he died, paradoxically, of blood poisoning. In a measure, however, he had prepared the way for the discovery of the sources of communicable diseases by Lord Joseph Lister and Louis Pasteur.

A *Textbook of Anatomy*, reprinted a score of times and bringing together the existing anatomical knowledge, won Joseph Hyrtl a secure place in the Vienna pantheon of medicine. A traditionalist in many ways, he cherished a conventional religious outlook and preferred to lecture in Latin; his carefully polished lectures sparkled with wit and grace. For the Vienna anatomical museum, Hyrtl greatly enlarged the collection of specimens. A father and son team at the Josephinum, Friedrich and Eduard Jaeger, made Vienna the most renowed center for the care and surgery of the eye in the world. A gifted and deft surgeon, Friedrich Jaeger had no peer as an ophthalmologist in his generation. Neither man wrote very much, yet both attracted crowds of students from foreign countries; the student record book of the Jaegers contains some fifteen hundred names, a seventh of them Americans.

The international eminence of Vienna in physiology derived directly from the researches of Ernst Wilhelm von Brücke on optics and on the borderland between physiology and physics. A dedicated investigator for whom science was a sacred calling, Brücke is credited with 140 scholarly papers and a prized two-volume book, *Lectures on Physiology*. He was honored by election as University rector, the first Protestant awarded that dignity, and by appointment to the Austrian House of Lords.

A versatile surgeon, Albert Christian Theodor Billroth, belongs among the giants in the medical annals of the second half of the nineteenth century. Trained in Berlin, he achieved world-wide fame with a *General Surgical Pathology and Therapeutics*, printed in many editions and extensively translated. He moved in 1867 from Zurich to Vienna where he stimulated his colleagues to research and teach. Billroth performed bold and original operations on the larynx and genital organs and perfected techniques for gastrointestinal surgery. Students were divided about his effectiveness as a lecturer, but when he turned down an invitation to take a chair in Berlin, a host of students in academic costumes, carrying torches and the old University flag, marched behind a band to the home of Billroth where they serenaded their mentor with the medieval student song "Gaudeamus igitur" and a hymn specially composed for the occasion. "What has given me the greatest joy in a diversified life," Billroth remarked toward the close of his distinguished career, "has been the foundation of a school which is continuing the trend of my activities alike in scientific and humanitarian directions, so that it seems destined to have a fair measure of durability." It did.

Theodor Hermann Meynert, primarily a brain anatomist, helped to lay the groundwork of a new branch of medicine, psychiatry. Skeptical of the assumption that victims of malignant mental afflictions were bewitched, he wished to find the physical basis of such derangements. The first Viennese psychiatrist of distinction, Meynert trained in his clinic many workers who advanced significantly the care and treatment of mental illness. He taught Sigmund Freud, for example, and had Arthur Schnitzler, best known as an imaginative writer, as an assistant in his clinic.

It would be easy to extend this survey of Viennese discoverers of new knowledge and new methods in medical science, but enough has been said to account for the distinction of the old city on the Danube in the sphere of healing. From all over the world young physicians trooped to the Hapsburg capital to deepen their medical knowledge and understanding. Study in Vienna became, indeed, a sort of international cult, not least among American practitioners, who made the city a "conventional Mecca."

Medical training in the United States was elementary and very inadequate, and quackery was a national shame. Thanks to its excellent teachers, clinical facilities, and abundant opportunities to handle or observe patients (and a comparatively cheap place to live), Vienna exerted a strong attraction upon American doctors who took the science of medicine seriously. It has been estimated (exaggeratedly, no doubt) that in the course of the nineteenth century ten thousand young American physicians went to Vienna for postgraduate instruction, and that twice as many more attended clinical courses lasting a month or a trifle longer or benefited from private teaching by tutors.

Aside from instruction, Viennese professors helped to advance the practice of medicine in the United States in other ways. For example, University specialists went to America either to treat patients (some wealthy Americans traveled to Vienna for treatment) or to offer courses, and the text books and scientific writings of Viennese experts were made available in translation. Besides, Viennese physicians who settled in America contributed to improvement in professional standards.

The immense prestige of the Vienna school of medicine and surgery overshadowed the accomplishments of other scientists, some of whom, however, earned international recognition. The geologist and physical geographer Eduard Suess won renown by regional studies on the structure of the Andes and other mountains and on the prehistoric linkage of Europe with northern Africa. He was still better known for *The Face of the Earth*, a monumental synthesis of the geology, physiography, and paleontology of the globe; this classic stimulated research in physical geography at many intellectual centers. Suess is also remembered as the principal promoter of the project to supply Vienna with water from the Alps.

Half-chemist, half-inventor, Carl Auer von Welsbach, born and educated for the most part in Vienna, engaged in basic researches on rare earths and originated a conical gauze mantle which converted gas into an intense incandescent light. For a while the Welsbach mantle gave lighting with gas a boost, but electricity presently became a formidable competitor. Fundamental contributions to theoretical physics, notably to the kinetic theory of gases, were made by Ludwig Boltzmann, whom the municipal government characteristically commemorated by placing his name on a street. Knowledge of astronomy was importantly extended by the studies of Theodor von Oppolzer, one of a galaxy of accomplished Vienna searchers of the heavens, who ingeniously calculated the paths of planets and comets and worked out a table on eclipses as far as the middle of the twenty-second century.

Teachers coming down from Germany, who accented the historical approach to jurisprudence, diverted legal scholarship in Vienna into fresh and stimulating channels. During a four year tenure in Vienna Rudolf von Jhering (or Ihering) shook legal studies to their very foundations—his influence persisted for a full generation after his return to Germany. Blessed with an original and richly stored mind and instructed by researches in Roman law, Jhering freely disclosed what that mind thought. He struck out with abandon against pedantic attachment to legal terminology and stiff formalism, contending that law should be applied so as to elevate human morality and dignity; to his way of thinking, the interests of society took precedence over property rights. In an exciting, widely circulated lecture on *The Battle for Right*, Jhering argued that every citizen should fight for his inalienable rights, and that if those rights are trespassed upon or denied, the human personality has been violated. Small wonder that the benches of his lecture hall were filled with progressively oriented students and unenrolled burghers, and loud were the lamentations when he forsook the Danubian capital for the University of Göttingen.

Spoken of as the "Austrian Aristotle," Franz C. Brentano infused lively currents into the rather stuffy atmosphere of

Vienna philosophy in the narrow and precise sense of the term. Thoroughly versed in the metaphysics of Aristotle and of the eminent scholastic doctors of medieval Catholicism, Brentano was also profoundly affected by the writings of the French positivist Auguste Comte, who endeavored to elaborate his theories into a scientific ethical and social system, and by England's John Stuart Mill. As Brentano saw matters, mental phenomena could be classified in three categories: the entertainment of ideas, the expression of judgments, and the display of emotional attitudes like love and hate. That analysis—and much else—he incorporated in *Psychology from the Empirical Standpoint* (1874); and he pleaded forcefully for the separation of psychology from its traditional ties with philosophy. While he acknowledged the value of Christian ethical principles, he also believed that the Deity must be thought of as a changing and not as a static concept. Although consistently theistic, Brentano was hotly castigated by Roman Catholic churchmen, which actually enhanced his attractiveness and helped to crowd his lecture hall not only with students but with gray-bearded professorial colleagues as well.

Professors of economics at Vienna gave the name of "the Austrian School" to a body of doctrine that attracted universal attention. Studying the intricate problems of value and price from the point of view of the consumer, the Vienna scholars stressed the subjective factor in determining value; for them economics stood closer to psychology than to history or mathematics. They propounded the theory of marginal utility, that is, an article possessed marginal utility when it was the last unit that an owner would sell and a customer would puchase, or, in the phrasing of an exponent of the theory, "the enjoyment derived from the least enjoyable unit is what we understand by final utility."

The founder of the "Austrian School," Karl Menger, published his most important book *The Principles of Economics* at the age of thirty-one. Therein he explained that he was concerned to ascertain "the law of price formation," and he set out in detail the concept (or law) of marginal utility; in subsequent writings, Menger energetically defended his reasoning against all opponents, of which there were many. For three decades he proved himself an exceptionally stimulating university lecturer in economic theory and public finance. "His ideas seem to come to him as he speaks," reported an American who sat at Menger's feet, "and are expressed in language so clear and simple . . . that it is a pleasure to follow him."

Where Menger led his most persuasive and devoted disciple, Eugen Böhm-Bawerk followed in diffusing the seed principles of the Vienna group. His major book, *Capital and Interest*, comprehensively and with literary brilliance analyzed the private enterprise pattern of economy; psychological factors he believed molded ideas on capital and interest. Students of Böhm-Bawerk, who ranked him among the immortals of economic theory, applauded his *Karl Marx and the Close of His System*—a premature title to say the least. This learned and trenchant polemic disputed the labor theory of value of Marx and indeed the whole corpus of his anticapitalist thought. From the University seminar of Böhm-Bawerk young men went forth, some to become prominent theoreticians of private capitalism and others, no less spirited, to become exponents of the Marxian creed. Like Menger, only more so, Böhm-Bawerk seized opportunities to apply his talents to current public problems, serving on three occasions as Austrian finance minister.

At the mid-nineteenth century, fresh winds began to blow through Viennese historical research and writing. New university chairs were authorized and professionally trained scholars, emulating their counterparts in Germany, aspired to elevate historiography to the dignity of a science. The opening in 1854 of the School (later the Institute) of Austrian Historical Research stands as a landmark in Viennese study of the past. Its eventual director, Theodor von Sickel, who had been trained in Germany and in Paris, practiced the most exacting standards of scholarship and taught them to a carefully chosen set of students, who became research specialists, archivists, and librarians.

The rich documentary resources of the Austrian court and state archives and lesser repositories at Vienna were opened to qualified investigators to an unprecedented extent by Alfred von Arneth, who in 1868 became custodian of the archival treasure house. By reason of stupendous feats in historiography Arneth achieved international recognition—a life of Prince Eugene of Savoy, an encyclopedic biography of the Empress Maria Theresa, and her correspondence with her numerous progeny.

A respected school of archaeology was established by F. A. Otto Benndorf, professor of classical archaeology at the University. He conducted research expeditions in Austria and excavations in the Balkan Peninsula and in Asia Minor, especially at Ephesus. Moreover, teams under his direction amassed considerable new knowledge about the mammoth palace of the Roman Emperor Diocletian at

Spalato (Split) in Dalmatia and made valuable finds at Carnuntum, an ancient camp and settlement of the Romans, an hour away from Vienna.

An illustrious professor of linguistics, Franz von Miklosic, the first teacher in Slavic philology at the University, is widely, if not universally, judged to hold the foremost rank among scholars who devoted themselves to understanding the languages of the Slavic-speaking peoples. Not only did he place the discipline of comparative Slav languages on firm foundations, but he uncovered new information on the Rumanian language and on the origins and customs of the mysterious gypsies. Fertile in research, gifted for appreciating languages in large perspective, and devoid of bias in study or writing, Miklosic belonged among Vienna's most exciting minds. Until after the First World War scholars in Vienna showed relatively little interest in the English language or in the literature of that tongue, which meant, as well, that learned interest in the United States was tepid at best.

It will be appropriate to round off this chapter with some consideration of the state of religion in Vienna after the mid-century. A statistical analysis disclosed that the Roman Catholic proportion of the population dropped from nearly 94 per cent in 1857 to just under 88 per cent in 1890; followers of Judaism, on the other hand, increased in the same period from a little more than 3 per cent to over 9 per cent, while the Protestant communions of Luther and Calvin of about 3 per cent registered no significant change. What statistics could not reveal of course was the disparity between observant and nominal communicants of the several faiths.

The Viennese were noted, and had long been noted, for fidelity to Mother Church. Their Catholicism, it is fair to say, possessed an easygoing, a distinctively humane quality, in contrast with the austere, ascetic, disciplined practice in Madrid, for instance. Church bells, pealing at six o'clock on Sunday morning, summoned streams of worshipers, carrying blue or red prayer books to divine worship. "In no city," remarked a careful British observer, "do the people attend more punctually on Sunday to their religious devotions." Mass pilgrimages to Catholic shrines likewise testified to popular piety; frequently, thousands of Viennese in a band, barefooted and staffs in hand, trudged ninety miles to the Styrian market town of Maria Zell, whose church sheltered a miracle-working image of the Virgin.

Evidence accumulated, on the other hand, to suggest increasing laxity in Roman Catholic observance. Gathering secularism in an urban environment, advances in the kingdom of knowledge, the ever wider diffusion of the rational and scientific spirit, with which were associated anticlericalism and religious indifference, wrought immeasurably upon the Christian heritage. Nevertheless, Roman Catholicism continued to exercise a powerful impact upon Viennese life in ministering to the spiritual needs of a large part of the population and as an instrument of social control. It was no light challenge for churchmen to adjust to the unparalleled conditions thrown up by the rapid growth of population and the constant streams of immigration. Statistically again, at 1900 Vienna had nearly 100 Roman Catholic parishes, 187 chapels, and 45 houses of religious orders, whose three thousand monks and nuns were for the most part engaged in teaching and nursing the sick. With unflagging zeal, learned professors in the Roman Catholic theological faculty at the University lectured and wrote on the doctrines of their creed.

Influential Catholic prelates interpreted the revolution of 1848 as "the judgment of God passed on thrones and peoples." To renew Catholicism, to strengthen the Church as a bulwark against extremism and as a defender of the prevailing political and social order, Austrian bishops met at Vienna in 1849 in solemn conference. From the deliberations issued a memorial to Franz Josef asking that the Catholic role in schooling be reinforced and that churchmen be granted more latitude in what they regarded as the proper sphere of religion. At the episcopal assembly the leading spirit was Joseph O. von Rauscher, an energetic ecclesiastical statesman and ardent Hapsburg, who had the ear of the Emperor, who was once his pupil.

Obedient to the mood of the conference, the crown decreed that prelates might apply to the Vatican for opinions on spiritual questions and order the punishment of refractory priests and that teachers of religion in public schools must be approved by a bishop. Beyond that, Franz Josef appointed Rauscher as special plenipotentiary to negotiate a treaty, or concordat, with the Vatican. That agreement, the Concordat of 1855, when concluded, assigned to the Pope the unrestricted right to appoint the archbishop of Vienna and to confirm Austrian bishops and certain lower churchmen nominated by the crown. It was also stated that the clergy would manage ecclesiastical properties and that religious orders were exempted from interference by civil authority. Church marriage was defined as obligatory for Catholics. Above all, the Concordat prescribed that Catholic beliefs should be imparted in schools, that bishops would supervise religious instruction and select the textbooks, and that they might forbid the reading of books deemed injurious to faith or morals.

The Concordat split articulate Vienna into two embattled camps. Anticlericals and the liberal press mercilessly attacked the concessions to the Church, contending that the fundamental principles of freedom of conscience and of state supremacy had been violated. Priest and dogma, it was said, had allied with police and sword to uphold authoritarianism and to perpetuate obscurantism. Denunciations became so widespread and bitter that the Catholic hierarchy instructed the parish clergy "to accustom their flocks gradually to the new order of things"; temporarily, the state censorship imposed clamps on the more outspoken critics.

As tokens of goodwill to militant anticlericalism the Emperor reduced the number of saint days to fifteen a year and authorized the small Protestant minority in Vienna to celebrate a Festival of the Reformation in place of its traditional Toleration Festival. For high Catholic ecclesiastics these decisions were gall and wormwood; but opponents of the Concordat would not rest until the pact they hated was dead and buried.

Eventually, the anticlerical forces achieved their main objectives. Guarantees of full religious freedom were embodied in the Austrian Constitution of 1867, and the parliament set up by that document whittled away the Concordat parcel by parcel. By one measure marriage was redefined as a civil contract and civil marriage was declared obligatory; legal cases involving marriage were removed from ecclesiastical jurisdiction. More important, the authority of churchmen in popular schooling was cut down almost to the vanishing point; they retained merely the right to pick school books to be used in teaching religion, which was noncompulsory in character. Jubilant Viennese anticlericals ratified the legislation in great street demonstrations.

Against the wishes of Rauscher, long since a cardinal, and other prominent Austrian prelates, the Vatican Council of 1870 proclaimed the dogma of papal infallibility, which furnished a formal basis for an imperial rescript canceling what remained of the Concordat. Subsequent enactments by parliament required that candidates for the priesthood must be acceptable to the civil authorities, levied taxes on the faithful to help defray ecclesiastical expenses, and permitted the suppression of monasteries and confiscation of their estates—a measure which the Emperor vetoed in effect.

The strong right arm of Rauscher, Johann R. Kutscher, who succeeded him as the archbishop of Vienna, was just as energetic in battling for ecclesiastical interests. But the public image of the Church took a turn for the better after 1881 when Coelestin J. Ganglbauer was installed as archbishop. Born into a peasant household, this conciliatory and urbane churchman belonged to the easygoing Benedictine monastic society. Rather surprisingly, in his enthronement address, he avoided any allusion to the anticlerical laws and referred sympathetically to science and progress. Ganglbauer heartily disapproved of the demagogic agitation of the clerically oriented Christian Socialists, who emerged late in the 1880's, and he practically ignored the wretchedness of the Viennese proletariat.

Leaders of the minority faiths in Vienna warmly applauded the clauses concerning freedom of conscience in the Constitution of 1867 and the abrogation of the Concordat. Protestants were accorded the right to set up a faculty of evangelical theology at the University. Wesleyan Methodists, on the other hand, were prohibited from holding public worship on the assigned reason that the sect had not been recognized by law; but that logic was not applied against the erection of an Anglican chapel adjoining the British Embassy. At 1900 adherents of Judaism maintained forty-two places of worship, a witness to the sharp rise in numbers; in them divergent ritualistic usages and interpretations of the faith, reformed and orthodox, persisted, with much the larger proportion in the traditional category.

ᦉ 4 ᦁ

cA Flowering of Culture

THE VIENNA of Franz Josef maintained its century-old standing as the musical capital of the world. Composers produced an astonishing quantity of high quality music and works in a lighter vein. True to tradition, the imperial court fostered good music in its chapel and rewarded star performers at the Imperial Opera with titles of honor and pensions, but more and more, the cultivated middle classes supplanted the aristocracy as patrons of musicians and music. Catholic churches also encouraged musical tastes in sacred Masses reflecting the humane Viennese attitude toward the faith, and under the direction of Salomon Sulzer, musicologist at the most fashionable reformed temple, Jewish religious music was significantly improved.

Thanks to a distinguished line of conductors, the Vienna Philharmonic Orchestra set artistic standards by which orchestras in other cities were judged. And the famous Society of the Friends of Music sponsored concerts, the choral Singing Society (it had a rival in the Singing Academy), and controlled the splendid conservatory, in which a number of composers and performers of international repute were trained. Societies named for individual composers, Viennese and foreign, offered concerts of their music and interpretative lectures; a ladies orchestra, begun in 1868, earned respect at home and on tours abroad.

Night after night, youths formed orderly queues at the opera house with the score of the current production in their hands and when the doors opened they dashed to their favorite seats (or standing places) in the fourth gallery. Performances that delighted younger spirits sometimes provoked hisses from traditionalists, leading on to rowdyism that obliged the police to intervene. Events in the Vienna world of music were discussed with animation in coffeehouses, shops, street cars; inscriptions on buildings announced that this or that musical celebrity had resided there and statues of great Viennese composers decorated public squares and parks.

Contemporary pictures show whole Vienna families playing music in the home, though few were able to afford pianos. Orchestras for dancing and concerts in public parks were very popular; folk tunes, waltzes, and marches were played by *Schrammel* quartets. The name recalled two brothers, Johann and Joseph Schrammel, violinists, who were joined by a guitar player and a fourth man with clarinet or accordion. Even hurdy-gurdies in Vienna ground out melodies of operas along with lighter fare! All classes delighted in folk songs in the dialect of the capital.

> *Human, Human, we're all human,*
> *Everyone has enough faults,*
> *We can't all be alike,*
> *So has Nature made us.*

Leading Vienna newspapers and magazines of art allocated a generous amount of space to music and performers. Of the professional critics, Eduard Hanslick, who contributed mostly to the *Neue Freie Presse*, was the most respected—and the most detested. Very opinionated and at times malicious he lashed out vigorously against the theories and creations of Richard Wagner, who in turn vilified the critic as unscrupulous and pernicious. For Johannes Brahms, on the other hand, Hanslick had a liking that amounted to reverence, and he stoked the flames of controversy between "Brahmins" and "Wagnerites." Hanslick collected his reviews in books which are invaluable sources of information on musical trends in the old Danubian capital; his excellent volume devoted to aesthetics, *On Musical Beauty*, ran through many editions and was translated into several languages.

Foreign musicians appeared in Vienna in an endless stream to conduct their works or to present recitals. Representative of them were the piano virtuoso Franz von Liszt, the cosmopolitan Giacomo Meyerbeer (whose *Huguenots* was an annual favorite), and the Frenchman Louis Hector Berlioz. *Cavalleria Rusticana* by Pietro Mascagni evoked such prolonged and enthusiastic applause at its première in Vienna that an encore was played, something seldom permitted. None of these geniuses, however, caused as much excitement—and quarreling—as the tragic, romantic, thunderous operas of Richard Wagner.

For Vienna Wagner developed warm affection, and at one point seriously thought of settling there. His productions from *Tannhäuser* through *Götterdämmerung* invariably called forth impassioned applause and fierce denunciations. Partisans in Vienna of the Bayreuth master and his detractors indulged in personal insults, family feuds, and raucous eruptions in coffeehouses. When Wagner adopted a vegetarian diet, as the way to regenerate mankind, and spoke out against Jewry, his mesmerized Viennese admirers imitated him.

Since Wagner derided the works of Brahms as old-fashioned, the creations of "the eunuch of music," Wagnerites thought so too. Like Ludwig van Beethoven, whose heir he is sometimes called, Brahms emigrated from Germany to Vienna, making it his home for thirty-seven years. Resourceful and prolific, Brahms composed symphonies and sonatas, choral and chamber pieces, and gypsy-inspired tunes during his residence in what he described as "the musicians' Holy City." The majestic *German Requiem*, reflecting personal bereavements, especially the death of his mother, consolidated the reputation of the composer with "Brahmins." The most extensive of his instrumental productions, the rhythmical *Concerto in B Major* for piano, earned a place on repertories the world over. By the test of originality, the structurally superb and melodic *Fourth Symphony* belongs among the classics of German music. In Vienna and abroad Brahms appeared in piano recitals and less frequently as a conductor.

Up to a point, Brahms had a competitor in the person of Karl Goldmark, Hungarian in origin, who went to Vienna to study the violin and matured as a composer of orchestral compositions and chamber music. Probably he is best known for the overture to *Sakuntala*, which has charmed generations of concertgoers, but experts in opera award him higher marks for the *Queen of Sheba*, glowing with lavish color and warm characterizations of personalities. If he had lived in almost any other city, Adelbert von Goldschmidt would doubtless have enjoyed far greater appreciation than he did. As it was, in spite of the many artistically excellent songs that he created and a fine secular cantata, *The Seven Deadly Sins,* he was rather dwarfed in Vienna by the array of distinguished writers of music.

Another Vienna master, the son of a village school-master, Anton Bruckner, adhered to homespun habits of living throughout his life. Observance of the Catholic faith verged on an obsession with him. "If the nearby bells tolled," one of his students remembered, "he would either fall on his knees in the midst of a class lesson and pray or, more often, would leave us and rush over to the Church for his devotions."

Sacred compositions, large and small, by Bruckner, best of all the *Mass in D Major* and *Te Deum,* and chamber and organ music and chorus works won permanence in the library of serious music. But his nine symphonies, the *Seventh* above all, simple yet profound, accounted for the immense international prestige Bruckner acquired. So much energy and time were consumed in teaching or as court organist and on concert trips that his productivity as a composer suffered. Yet Bruckner was the first composer to be awarded an honorary degree by the University of Vienna; his applications for similar distinctions at the universities of Pennsylvania and Cincinnati met negative responses.

No Viennese composer was more influenced by Wagner than Hugo Wolf, an Austrian provincial who came to the capital with the conviction that he was destined to write music that would endure. Despite its boisterous orchestra-tion, the symphonic poem *Penthesilea* would probably have assured Wolf a place among the leading composers of his generation. He world renown, however, rests upon melodious songs for voice and piano which he wrote in amazing quantity—more than a hundred in a single year.

He worked at such a fantastic pace that his mind became deranged, and he died at the age of forty-three.

The foremost Vienna conductor of the period, Hans Richter, carried the Philharmonic Orchestra into its golden era, and he also served as conductor at the opera and the court chapel. While he lived, this imposing personality grew into a legend; his musical interests ranged widely, though he had small taste for contemporary compositions. London lured him away, as Boston did his colleague, Wilhelm Gericke. With this talented musician in charge the newly founded Boston Symphony reached a high level of performance, and Gericke exerted an inestimable influence on music of quality in the United States generally.

No teacher of piano in Vienna equalled Theodor Leschetizky, who is credited with innovations that stressed the importance of wrists as well as the fingers in piano playing. A rigorous disciplinarian and a stickler for detail, he attracted students from everywhere, the daughter of Mark Twain among them; Ignace Paderewski was no doubt his most celebrated pupil.

As nothing else, the music of Johann Strauss the Younger molded the mythical international image of Vienna as a gay, fairy-tale community, whose inhabitants lived remote from everyday realities. Strauss attributed his marvelous productivity to the inspiration of the Danubian capital. "If it is true that I have talent," he remarked, "I owe it above everything else to my beloved city, Vienna . . . . In its soil is rooted my whole strength, in its air float the melodies which my ear has caught, my heart has drunk in, and my hand has written down. My Vienna, the city of song and spirit." Melodious waltzes, Strauss explained, gushed out like clear water, some of them celebrating contemporary events like the tearing down of the ancient Vienna fortifications and the merger of the outer suburbs with the rest of the community.

On some evenings "the Waltz King" conducted bands in five or more places! To dispel the gloom occasioned by a disheartening military defeat by Prussia in 1866, Strauss composed "The Beautiful Blue Danube," whose bewitching cadences have captivated audiences everywhere, and its frivolous lines have done a good deal to nourish the legend of frolicsome Vienna.

> *Vienna, be gay!*
> *And what for, pray?*
> *A glimmer of light—*
> *With us it's night,*
> *Carnival's come!*
> *Ho-ho, ha-hum,*
> *Well, why court sorrow?*
> *There's still to-morrow,*
> *So laugh and be merry.*

Apart from waltzes, Strauss composed a profusion of operettas—sixteen finished ones—generally light and merry, though not devoid of philosophical implications. The masterpiece, *Die Fledermaus*, subtly recaptured the atmosphere and tastes of Viennese bourgeois society and its intoxicating arias have hypnotized listeners all over the globe. Strauss' second most popular operetta, *The Gypsy Baron*, replete with exotic music and fanciful romanticism, recalled the era of Maria Theresa.

Strauss undertook a memorable trip to the United States in 1872, conducting at Boston and New York. Becoming the darling of the New World, as of the Old, he saluted America with the "New Jubilee Waltz," featuring a sparkling arrangement of the Star Spangled Banner in waltz time.

Opera for the popular stage had two other prolific and noteworthy practitioners, Franz von Suppé and Karl Millöcker. A Dalmatian of Italian stock, Suppé, the closest approach to Strauss in technical stature, achieved distinction with *Fatinitza*; except for the overture to *The Poet and Peasant*, his orchestral productions never attracted much attention outside of Austria. Catchy tunes in the *Student Beggar* and *The North Light* brought lasting recognition to Millöcker.

Excellent orchestral ensembles and choruses enriched the cultural life of Vienna in the Wagner-Strauss era. And the sumptuous new opera house provided the setting for improved productions, while the installation of electric lighting (1887) made possible novel theatrical effects. Several internationally famous prima donnas graced the Vienna operatic stage. Outstanding were the soprano Pauline Lucca, whose acting compensated for what her voice lacked in expressiveness, the highly dramatic soloist Bertha Ehnn, the soprano Lilli Lehmann, who brilliantly executed difficult Wagnerian roles, and Adelina Patti, who, Hanslick thought, was "gifted with the most musical of voices and the utmost of musical talent." There were also the richly gifted and charming Marie Geistinger, who excelled in Strauss operettas, enthralling audiences in America as in Vienna, and her beautiful rival, Josephine Gallmeyer, whose mimicry in comedy situations evoked peals of laughter; she came off less effectively in sober productions and had only limited success on a visit to the United States.

Alexander Girardi, the best loved male performer, often played alongside of Geistinger in operettas and made a big hit as a character actor.

The magnificent, splendidly equipped new Burgtheater opened a fresh chapter in the history of the Vienna stage. Playwrights coveted the honor of having a production presented here, and actors and actresses trained at the Burgtheater obtained engagements in Europe and overseas. By a good margin top honors for acting belonged to Adolf von Sonnenthal, excellent in both tragic and comic roles. He had his most conspicuous success—in Europe and the United States—as Nathan in *Nathan the Wise*, a drama by Gotthold E. Hessing teaching the virtue of tolerance.

Playing the same role, Frederick Mitterwurzer, after three attempts, managed to get a firm foothold in the Burgtheater. Critics likened his performance in *Hamlet* to that of the English actor David Garrick, and he also interpreted Albrecht von Wallenstein and acted in plays by Henrik Ibsen and Hermann Sudermann with great success; on a guest tour to the United States, press critics showered Mitterwurzer with enthusiastic praise. His premature death robbed the Vienna stage of a very accomplished entertainer.

The brilliant tragedienne, Charlotte Wolter, won universal recognition as the foremost personality in her profession. Her repertory was extensive, and she was at her finest when playing Cleopatra or Messalina, attired in glamorous costumes designed by Hans Makart. She also starred in title roles created by the Viennese playwrights Franz Grillparzer and Christian F. Hebbel, commented on below. While still a girl, Stella Hohenfels moved from triumph to triumph on the stage and in a long theatrical career thrilled critics and patrons by scintillating performances in a dozen different roles.

By reason of extraordinary emotional qualities, a magnetic personality and a beautiful voice, Katharine Schratt ranked with the leading actresses of the period. Franz Josef learned to admire this genial and vivacious lady, and in his later years developed a close, discreet companionship with her that lasted until his death; so intimate in fact was the Emperor with the former reigning beauty at the Burgtheater that Viennese wits tagged him "Herr Schratt." Whenever Sarah Bernhardt, greatest French tragic actress, made an appearance in Vienna, she was assured of a rapturous reception.

The theater, like music, was the subject of daily and impassioned discussion by the press and public of Vienna. Whether at the *Theater an der Wien*, the new Ronacher theater, or suburban playhouses, managers chose plays calculated to appeal generally as well as offerings for the sophisticated minority. Satirical farces of an older Vienna preserved their popularity, and newer, more mature, and weightier productions attracted theatergoers.

The finest of Viennese dramatists, Franz Grillparzer, who had made his reputation before the mid-nineteenth century, added thereafter a distinctly original play, *Esther*, full of interesting allusions to the current Austrian scene. *The Brothers Feud in the House of Hapsburg*, dramatizing the early phases of the Thirty Years' War, made its way into theatrical repertories after the death of Grillparzer. A grateful Vienna remembered the accomplishments of its foremost man of letters in a handsome monument placed in the *Volksgarten*; charming bas-reliefs recall scenes from his most prized plays.

Dramatic literature was permanently enriched by Christian F. Hebbel, who moved to Vienna from Germany at middle age. He pioneered in penetrating psychological interpretations of prevailing manners and moral standards in both polite and proletarian society. In his masterpiece, the vividly written and structurally admirable *Agnes Bernauer,* Hebbel taught that the interests of society as a whole transcended individual interests. Certain specialists hold that he was at his best in *Die Nibelungen,* a long epic based upon ancient German folklore. In perspective the works of Hebbel are regarded as foreshadowing the psychological and social drama cultivated so effectively by Henrik Ibsen.

The melodramatic *Priest of Kirchfeld* by Ludwig Anzengruber brilliantly depicted the comic and the tragic elements in Austrian rural living, and its anticlerical tone assured it a triumphant reception at a time when the campaign against the Concordat of 1855 was in full spate. In *The Fourth Commandment* Anzengruber faithfully exposed the harsh and the sordid in the daily round of little men in Vienna, and exploited with exactness the primitive vernacular of the capital. High-grade comedy had a master in Eduard von Bauernfeld, who skillfully blended political with social satire. The forty plays that he produced were presented over a thousand times during his life.

Except for drama, Viennese literature of the period had little significance. No novels of importance appeared, though the voluminous writings of the priest and social reformer, Ludwig Donin, attracted a large readership. His Catholic emphases, as in *The Life and Deeds of God,* are believed to have exerted considerable influence on the habits of many ordinary Viennese.

Architecture flourished in Vienna during the four decades after the mid-century, native-born talents competing with rivals from northern Europe. Whereas in the Middle Ages architects had raised great structures like St. Stephen's and the Hofburg and in the eighteenth century baroque churches and palaces, in the latest age thought and energy were invested in the great public architecture along the new Ringstrasse, befitting the capital city of a populous and extensive realm. Advancing industrialism had expression, to be sure, in mansions for the plutocracy, in factories and railway stations, and in banking and office buildings.

Architectural conservatism distinguished the monumental structures that were erected along the Ring. Two professors, Eduard van der Nuell and August von Siccardsburg, designed the opera house in French, or Neo-Renaissance, style. Pairs of rectangular wings project on each side toward the rear, and the structure is crowned with an immense curved roof; painters and sculptors lavishly embellished the foyers, corridors, and staircases. Nearly 2,500 patrons could be accommodated in the magnificent auditorium, though it was somewhat deficient in length, the box reserved for the imperial family being less than a hundred and fifty feet from the stage. Critics lampooned the opera house as "a Waterloo of architecture," and sensitive soloists haughtily announced that they would not sing in the "monstrosity." Upset by criticisms, Van der Nuell committed suicide.

Danish-born Theophilus E. von Hansen, designed several splendid Viennese structures, such as the home of the

Society of the Friends of Music and the Academy of Fine Arts, both on the model of the Italian Renaissance. Hansen also planned the *Bourse*, or stock exchange, and was responsible for several palaces and commercial buildings of which the Heinrichshof across the Ring from the opera house may be taken as a representative example. Its elaborate Renaissance façade, fine lines and proportions invited considerable imitation in European cities. Hansen drew upon Byzantine styles in creating an interesting church for the Orthodox Greeks, and classical Greece inspired his plans for the parliament building, the supreme glory of his career. Leading up to the portico, which has imposing Corinthian columns, are statues of eminent historians of antiquity and representations in bronze of men training horses.

A short distance away stands the massive Neo-Gothic *Rathaus*, or city hall, the handiwork of Friedrich Schmidt. Covering five acres, this huge structure has a central tower, 320 feet high, surmounted by a tall knight brandishing a long sword. Side wings end in a high pavilion with a dull mansard roof; arcades encircle a fine central court, and there are half a dozen smaller courts. The interior of this showpiece of the "New Vienna" contains two grand staircases leading to a large festival chamber and five hundred rooms and halls to accommodate the needs of the municipal administration.

As was so true of his contemporaries, the thinking of Baron Heinrich von Ferstel was deep rooted in architectural traditions. In open competition he obtained the contract to design the *Votivkirche*, a memorial to the escape of Franz Josef from assassination (1853). No more perfect Gothic edifice was built anywhere in the nineteenth century. Two lofty towers distinguish the noble façade, and within there is a wealth of beautiful stained glass windows and sculptured monuments. For the new University Ferstel chose the style of the Italian Renaissance; this big quadrangular structure surrounds a pretty courtyard with arcades. Stately Corinthian columns and allegorical ceiling paintings are features of the entry hall; lecture and seminar rooms and faculty studies are located in the wings, and a fireproof library stretches across the rear, all approached by finely arranged staircases.

Two great museums of art and natural history along the Ring are primarily the products of Karl von Hasenauer, assisted by Gottfried Semper in preparing the designs. The structures, which reflect the influence of Italian Renaissance architecture, are almost identical and stand on opposite sides of a large square. A lofty, prim façade fronts on a massive central block, with a wing on either side, and an octagonal dome is crowned with a colossal Greek figure. Despite odd cupolas and excessive ornamentation, the museums compare worthily with buildings having similar functions elsewhere in the Western World. The grand staircase of the art gallery has steps of white marble and pillars of varicolored marble, garishly gilded; pretentious marble walls and floors are laid out in checkerboard patterns. Paintings transferred from state galleries or from garret storage closets were exhibited in spacious, well-lighted rooms. Masterpieces of art, such as portraits by Velázquez and rare treasures of the early Flemish and Venetian Renaissance schools, were displayed, as were innumerable canvases of dubious value.

Into the museum of natural history were gathered rich collections of minerals, fossils, and antiquities, illustrating the passage of man from prehistoric times into the imperial Roman centuries and the progress of peoples outside of Europe toward refined ways and manners, along with birds, fish, mammals, and plants.

Baroque touches figure in the essentially late Renaissance architecture of the new Burgtheater, designed by Hasenauer and Semper. A spacious foyer passes all around the interior of this marvel of theatrical construction, and the auditorium has no pillars so that every patron has an unobstructed view of the stage. Originally, the auditorium, which seats two thousand, was laid out in the form of a lyre, but caustic criticisms forced rearrangement. The theater was equipped with unique lighting and heating facilities, novel safety precautions against fire, and mechanical devices for moving scenery. Settings for plays were prepared in a deep space beneath the stage—a section of the old city moat—and sent up as required. Opened in 1888, the theater attracted world-wide attention in architectural and theatrical circles. With the completion of the Burgtheater the spacious age of Ringstrasse architecture practically came to an end.

Sculpture and painting in the Danubian capital showed greater originality than architecture. Public squares and new parks afforded ample opportunities for workers in bronze and marble to display their gifts. Sculpture in Vienna, which had languished for generations, entered a new era with the arrival in 1840 of Anton D. von Fernkorn, who, like so many other men who shaped Viennese cultural life, was reared and received his professional training in Germany. His outstanding creations are two bronze equestrian statues on marble pedestals in the Square of Heroes before the Hofburg. The ensemble of the memorial to the

Archduke Charles, hero of an inconclusive victory over Napoleon in 1809, is extremely good; the head of the horse is perfect, but the forelegs are too long and the tail much too heavy. Ennobled for this piece, Fernkorn proceeded to carve a counterpart to it in honor of Prince Eugene of Savoy. Although the figure of the Prince is remarkably well done, it is a gross distortion representing him as a giant, whereas in fact he was small and spare. The forepart of the horse comes off admirably, but the hind legs and tail are monstrosities.

The masterpiece of Kaspar C. von Zumbusch is a dignified monument to the Empress Maria Theresa in the square between the art gallery and the museum of natural history. The great Empress sits enthroned at the summit of a tall granite shaft; at the foot her field marshals ride on bronze horses and her statesmen stand guard. Near the top, niches hold representations of eminent musicians and intellectuals of the period. Zumbusch also designed a noble figure of Beethoven, though allegorical reliefs at the base are hardly in good taste.

After Fernkorn and Zumbusch, the ablest of the Viennese sculptors, was Viktor O. Tilgner who produced a first-rate statue of Mozart and less distinguished memorials of Bruckner, the composer, and Makart, the painter. He first came into prominence with a splendid bust in the baroque manner of the tragedienne Charlotte Wolter. An interesting though poorly proportioned white marble statue of Franz Schubert stands out among the monuments of celebrities erected in the city park. A product of Karl Kundmann, the large seated figure gives the impression of a tall, well-formed man, whereas the famous poet of music was in fact short and stumpy. Reliefs on the pedestal are absurd allegories in no way suggestive of the simple, yet mystical tastes of the very human musician.

From the Kundmann studio also came an unusual monument in memory of Admiral Wilhelm von Tegetthoff, who destroyed Italian seapower in a war in 1866. Placed at the approach to the Prater, it is a tall marble column, from which project the prows of battleships, topped by the Admiral, telescope in hand. An arresting pyramid of red Swedish granite commemorates Mayor Johann A. Liebenberg, who presided over Vienna during the Turkish siege of 1683. Raised on a site across from the University where a decisive encounter with the attacking Turks took place, the obelisk contains a relief bust of the mayor and is decorated with allegorical devices recalling the epochal victory of the Christian forces.

After the mid-century painting in Vienna as well as sculpture attained unsurpassed levels of popularity, though little known outside of the Danubian region. The monumental architecture of the period colored the outlook of artists who painted very large historical canvases or applied themselves to decorating profusely the new public structures. Freshly realistic portraits of the aristocratic and the affluent mainly and wonderful landscapes were also cultivated in Vienna, not a few of whose creative workers responded to impressionistic currents emanating from Paris.

At the outset of the period the most esteemed painters had established reputations earlier, like Ferdinand G. Waldmüller whose tireless brush created over a thousand pieces. This genial darling of fashionable Viennese society turned out portraits, possessing photographic realism with dashes of imaginative fancy, and brightly colored landscapes of the Prater and the Danubian countryside. Joseph R. von Führich, a devout Roman Catholic who specialized in church decoration, intended through his art to teach the dogmas of the faith and to quicken the allegiance of believers. He reached a high point in sacred painting in seven murals for the vestibule of the Altlerchenfeld Church, six of them depicting the creation and the last showing the Creator at rest on the seventh day. While Führich concentrated on service to the Church, Moritz von Schwind applied his talents to secular ornamentation, above all to the opera house; fancying gay romantic figures, he painted frescoes whose motifs were inspired by Mozart's *The Magic Flute.*

Having made a name for himself by ornamentation of the Greek Orthodox Church by Hansen, Karl H. Rahl set to work on the adornment of Ringstrasse structures. A lover of color and of historical and allegorical paintings in large dimensions, Rahl's tastes attained rather general vogue. His portrait of the sculptor Adam Rammelmayer possesses a Rembrandt quality. Quantities of portraits came from the brush of Hans Canon, as he is known by his pseudonym. Broadening out, Canon painted gigantic pictures to decorate the University and the museum of natural history, such as "The Cycle of Life" for the ceiling of the latter. It is an overloaded production with dozens of figures representing varied aspects of the human pageant. At the top, for instance, two intensely realistic warriors mounted on fiery steeds prepare to strike death blows at each other, while at the base an elderly seer rests his hand serenely on an hourglass.

Passion for the colossal and lavish use of color were carried to extravagant heights by Hans Makart, supreme arbiter of Viennese taste in painting of the 1870's. A native of Salzburg, he never lost the fondness for baroque sumptuousness that he acquired in his boyhood environment; as a youth he quickly made a reputation for himself and settled in Vienna as a recognized artist. He painted notable portraits of the star actress Charlotte Wolter and of aristocrats and plutocratic ladies. Gracefully shaped and voluptuous nude women were favorite themes of Makart ("The Chase of Diana" and, especially, "The Triumph of Ariadne"); prudish critics were prone to dismiss these pictures as erotic and disgustingly coarse, unworthy of an artist, who prided himself on his intellectual powers.

What appealed most to Makart, though, were large-scale historical paintings, like "The Entry of Charles V into Antwerp." This grandiose creation, riotous in coloring, teems with glittering costumes and scantily clad girls. The artist had abundant scope for his showmanship talents in a glamorous pageant which he arranged down to minute details in 1879 in connection with the twenty-fifth anniversary of the wedding of the Emperor and Empress. Admirers likened Makart to Rubens and Titian, though in fact his art was imitative, frivolous, and unskillful in draftsmanship.

A second devotee of exuberant coloring, August von Pettenkofen, preferred to paint contemporary instead of historical subjects. As an army officer, he was stationed at various points in the Monarchy and his canvases reflected that experience. He painted the exotic grandeur of the Hungarian plain, sleepy market towns, happy-go-lucky gypsy types, and military scenes. He loved, too, to make lithographs and illustrations for popular magazines.

Though only modestly appreciated while he lived, the

art of Michael Neder, a humble shoemaker, eventually gained an honored place in Vienna galleries. His best works were almost photographic representations of fellow proletarians, cheerful in spite of privations. "Tavern Scene," a typical example of Neder's painting, showed a jolly company of workmen, half of them lustily applauding a pair of fiddlers while the others play cards under the inquisitive gaze of a serving girl.

Versatile Anton Romako, pupil and disciple of Rahl, created glowing rural landscapes, portraits noted for beauty of facial expression ("The Family of the Artist at Breakfast"), and big historical scenes ("The Coming of Marcus Aurelius to Vienna"). His impressionistic leanings irritated the reigning Makart, but had some influence on the rising generation of Vienna artists. With the death of Romako in 1889, a notable period in the culture of Vienna in general virtually came to an end. Younger, more cosmopolitan spirits waited eagerly to divert the fine arts and literature into new and exciting channels.

ᴥঌ 5 ঌᴥ

The ᴄAscendancy of Christian Socialism

$F_{OUR\ NEW}$ secular creeds—Pan-Germanism, Christian Socialism, Social Democracy, and Zionism—competed for sympathy and support in the Vienna of the final decade of the nineteenth century and into the twentieth.

Pan-Germanism set as its goal the union of the predominantly German-peopled areas of Austria with the German Empire. A noisy, radical wing detested the Hapsburg dynasty and Roman Catholicism, and spoke out against the rising importance of Slavic and Jewish elements in the Viennese population. George von Schoenerer, a fiery-tempered and intensely chauvinistic rabble-rouser, best personified the Pan-German agitation. But personal jealousies and factionalism in the top echelon seriously crippled the Pan-German party, organized in 1890, as a political force.

Christian Socialism, staunchly devoted to the house of Hapsburg, identified Christianity with Roman Catholicism and the interests of clerical traditionalism. The "Socialism" in the name disclosed aversion to a laissez-faire economy and repudiation of historic Liberalism, as responsible for anticlerical legislation, secularization of schooling, and the hard times that followed the financial crash of 1873. Christian Socialism promised to protect the "little man" (the Austrian peasant included) against large com-

88

panies and to save the independent craftsman from extinction by the factory. Equating big business with Jewry, Christian Socialism wished to check the penetration of Jews into banking and industry—and also the learned professions, journalism, and the cultural arts.

Roman Catholic social reform currents abroad in Germany affected profoundly the philosophy of Baron Karl von Vogelsang, the spiritual and intellectual father of Austrian Christian Socialism. By birth a German Protestant aristocrat, Vogelsang embraced Catholicism and emigrated to Vienna, where in 1875 he assumed the editorship of the leading clerical organ, *Vaterland*. Through its columns and a monthly review on social questions, he thundered against Liberalism as harmful both to individuals and to the community as a whole.

Upon Catholicism rested a solemn duty, Vogelsang taught, to stand forth as the protector of the underprivileged and the oppressed, else they would take up with radicalism, perilous for public order. Laws to safeguard the interests of handicraftsmen, shopkeepers, and industrial wage earners should be shaped in keeping with Christian ideals of fairness, mutual co-operation, and humanity. His teaching hastened the welfare legislation of the 1880's and made a deep and lasting impression upon Viennese Catholic social thought.

A few high aristocrats were drawn into the Vogelsang orbit, of whom the most influential were the brothers Liechtenstein, Alfred and Alois, the latter more especially. Very wealthy, educated for the law, and cultivated, Alois devoted himself to social problems in writings and as a deputy in the Austrian parliament; he struck up a working alliance with the Vogelsang circle. Socially minded young

Viennese priests also aligned with the movement, as was the case with Rudolf F. Eichhorn, who investigated and vividly reported on social realities in the proletarian district which he served as priest. A revealing pamphlet from his pen about the "white slaves" at work on the Vienna street railways caused a sensation.

Conservative by tradition, the Catholic hierarchy took a dim view of Christian Socialism as demagogic and divisive of Church forces. That attitude shifted, however, in view of the Vatican stand on social problems. In 1891, the year after Vogelsang died, the victim of a street accident, Pope Leo XIII issued a famous encyclical, *Rerum novarum*, in which he, "the workingman's Pontiff," set forth his conception of the ideal social order, grounded on the principle of Church activity in the social sphere.

Christian Socialism, meantime, was developing into a potent political instrument under the driving dynamic of one of the most remarkable Viennese of the Franz Josef period, Karl Lueger, destined to become the most popular mayor that the Hapsburg capital had ever known. By origin, Lueger belonged to the class of little men; his forebearers were peasants and artisans, and his father was the custodian of a school building. At the age of twenty-six he emerged from the University with a doctorate in law, and he plunged into practice, rapidly earning respect in the profession. Called "Handsome Karl" because of his splendid presence, he possessed that intangible, magnetic quality of leadership known as charism. Into popular addresses he mixed a good deal of homely wit, spoken in the Vienna vernacular and with vehemence.

Elected to the city council as a Liberal in 1875, Lueger sat in that body with only a slight interruption until his death thirty-five years later. He quarreled with his Liberal colleagues, exposed corruption, and called stridently for franchise reform. Becoming an outspoken foe of big, moneyed interests, he also indulged in demagogic philippics against Jewry—a piece of Asia in Central Europe, he tagged it. About 1885, he manifested open sympathy with the views of Vogelsang, and in the autumn of 1888, he united with like-minded men in founding the Christian Socialist party.

At almost precisely the same time, a Social Democratic party was organized (1889), bringing together several varieties of anticapitalist doctrine, mostly Marxian. Unity was achieved at a conference convened in the pretty market village of Hainfeld, thirty miles away from Vienna. Under the influence of the corresponding party in Germany, which was preponderantly evolutionary, not revolutionary, the Austrians pressed for manhood suffrage, unfettered freedom for workers to form unions, a shorter workday, broader social welfare legislation, and removal of every vestige of clericalism from what they regarded as the secular sphere.

The outstanding Marxist was Victor Adler, son of a well-to-do-merchant, who in 1855 moved from Prague to Vienna. While practicing medicine, Adler learned of the hardships and grievances of the proletariat, and he dedicated himself to the betterment of that class. He was the key personality in bringing about the united Social Democratic party at the Hainfeld conference; and he helped to found the Social Democratic monthly *Die Zukunft*, a journal for intellectuals, and the *Arbeiter Zeitung*, which in 1895 began to appear every day. Party congresses, mass rallies, clubs of all sorts propagated the creed and aims of

Social Democracy, and secular trade unions were an invaluable ally of the party; Adler referred to them as the "Siamese twins."

The fourth novelty in Vienna public life was Zionism, which was dedicated to the achievement of a Jewish national state in ancient Palestine—then belonging to the Turkish empire—whither Jews might emigrate and live exempt from insults and indignities, without discrimination or harassment. This Messianic dream attained unexampled vitality through the labors of Theodor Herzl, saluted as "the second Moses." Coming from Budapest, his well-to-do family settled in Vienna in 1878, and he earned a law degree at the University. As a youth Herzl advocated assimilation of Jewry, even recommending mass Christian baptism; but his thinking changed, partly because of the incessant demagoguery in Vienna against the Jews.

Casting away the formula of assimilation, Herzl reasoned that the Jewish question was fundamentally a national problem that could only be resolved by the establishment of a Jewish homeland. Yet efforts to persuade affluent Viennese Jews and influential Hebrew spiritual leaders to his way of thinking fell flat. In a famous pamphlet, *The Jewish State* (1896), subtitled, "An Attempt at a Modern Solution of the Jewish Question," Herzl pleaded for an autonomous Jewish commonwealth and urged that political and financial agencies should be created to translate the homeland vision into reality.

A Zionist Congress held (1897) at Basel, Switzerland, set up an executive committee, composed of Herzl and four of his Vienna friends, and arranged for the publication of a Zionist newspaper and the founding of a bank. When the Turkish government rejected an application for a Jewish state in Palestine, Herzl negotiated with the British government for an alternative area of settlement. The London cabinet offered African Uganda, which Herzl thought should be accepted as a temporary haven, but Russian Zionist leaders, particularly, would hear of nothing but Palestine. Wrangling inside the organization hastened the death of Herzl (1904) at the age of only forty-four. But the impetus he had imparted to the cause gathered momentum, and forty-four years after his death the remains of the prophet were triumphantly moved from Vienna to Mount Herzl high above Jerusalem.

Long since, the Christian Socialists had supplanted the Liberal administration of Vienna. At municipal election after municipal election, the Lueger forces in the city council gained seats, passing the Liberal contingent in April of 1895, though an independent bloc held the balance of power. After another balloting further increased Christian Socialist strength, the council chose "Handsome Karl" for the high and responsible civic distinction of mayor. Bowing to the wishes of influential Liberals and of Hungarians, who were incensed by Christian Socialist denunciations of their senior politicians, Emperor Franz Josef declined to confirm the election of Lueger. The council was dissolved and management of the municipality was entrusted to an imperial commission. Yet subsequent verdicts at the polls gave still more seats to Christian Socialism. And after Lueger's fourth election as mayor, Franz Josef in April of 1897 grudgingly gave his assent. A new chapter in the public life of Vienna began.

Having vanquished Liberalism, Christian Socialism was confronted by a far more formidable adversary, Social Democracy. At Austrian parliamentary elections of 1897, the

93

first in which Socialists participated, the party polled eighty-eight thousand votes in Vienna (some thirty thousand fewer than the Christian Socialists). It is a plausible assumption that by the dawn of the new century, a majority of the politically articulate proletarians had entered the Marxist camp.

Conditions of labor and life in the thick-peopled industrial wards of Vienna swelled the Socialist forces. Wages for unskilled or semiskilled workmen hardly kept abreast of the rising costs of living; many men could not afford to found families, a situation that had bearing on the large, though declining, percentage of unmarried mothers. Regardless of what Austrian law prescribed, working hours in some shops and mills ran as high as seventeen daily.

The housing situation for wageworkers remained intolerably bad. As late as 1910 fewer than one Vienna flat in ten boasted a bathroom, and only about one in five had an inside toilet. Possibly a quarter of the households sublet sections of their cramped apartments or rented beds only to lodgers. The Danubian capital remained, as it had long been, a community of contrasts in which the privations and squalor of the proletarian mass contradicted the splendors of an affluent minority.

At last, in 1900, Socialist pressure secured a limited extension of the franchise to choose city councilmen. To the traditional three classes of electors, a fourth curia was added in which all adult males who had resided in Vienna at least three years were eligible to vote. Each of the first three categories, totalling about 52,000 in all, elected forty-six councilmen, while the fourth class with 228,000 voters chose only twenty. That arrangement was a far cry from equal suffrage, yet the franchise went unchanged until after the First World War. At the first election after the creation of the fourth class, proletarian wards sent two Socialists to the council, and five more seats were captured later. And, the imperial government extended the franchise to males over twenty-four for the election of deputies to the Austrian parliament. At the elections of 1907, under the new electoral law, Socialist candidates polled one third of the Vienna ballots, and their party emerged as the largest in the legislature.

A new ward, Brigittenau, meanwhile, had been carved out of an existing one, and in 1905 Florisdorf and adjacent villages on the left bank of the Danube were annexed to the capital, enlarging the area of the city by nearly half. The population increased by a half a million between 1891 and 1905, and five years later it passed the two million mark.

Lueger and his Christian Socialists faithful to pledges, proceeded to make the "Greater Vienna" a reality in more ways than mere geography, and to enhance its distinctive personality. As a starter, the municipality undertook to supply gas for the community, which a British-owned Continental Gas Company had been furnishing for over half a century. Borrowing from a Berlin bank, a city gas works was constructed and a second plant went into operation in 1911. Before that, a municipally-owned electricity works had been erected, and the interests of three private electric companies were bought out. Costs of utilities to consumers were reduced, service improved, and the use of electricity in homes very greatly extended.

At the same time, street railways were fully electrified, and lines were purchased by the municipality from private firms. More rapid service and less crowding in cars ensued;

trackage and passengers doubled in a few years. By 1902, a metropolitan line, whose route partly traversed the boulevard once occupied by the outer city walls, was finished. All in all, Vienna experienced a quick revolution in public transport. Communications were improved by the installation of more telephones, 36,000 being available by 1908. Gasoline-powered taxicabs appeared in 1899, the pioneer motorbus seven years later, and in 1910, 3,200 private automobiles and 2,600 motorcycles were licensed. A second radical change in transportation was in the making.

The Lueger administration overcame the inadequacies of the water supply which had been a decade-old headache for the city fathers—and mothers. A second great aqueduct conveyed water from the Styrian Alps, almost 113 miles away. Improvements were effected, too—in sewerage, in the paving and lighting of streets, and in widening streets, during the process of which many picturesque old landmarks in the inner city were toppled. The Danube was further regulated to prevent flooding, and another bridge was thrown across the river.

The municipality and philanthropic agencies increased the facilities to care for Viennese in distress. Outstanding were new hospitals, one of them for children only, new orphanages, and the Am Steinhof asylum (1907) for the mentally ill. This unusual institution resembled a miniature city covering nearly four hundred acres and had provisions to care for over 2,400 patients, who were assigned to pavilions in accordance with the nature of their malady. The grounds contained a church, a theater, a dance hall, and workshops. Noteworthy, too, was the Lainz Home for the Aged, another showpiece of the Greater Vienna; there as many as 3,400 indigent, elderly persons could be cared for in dignity and in cheerful surroundings.

Additional hostels, usually conducted by private societies, for apprentices and transient, rootless indigents were erected. Soup kitchens, in which the poor could purchase a noonday meal of soup, a small piece of meat with vegetable, and pudding for a few pennies, were extended, and public bathhouses increased. Moreover, the city government set up and maintained an employment bureau, an insurance company, and an inexpensive burial service; the vast Central Cemetery was beautified, and a chapel in it was dedicated just in time to receive the body of Mayor Lueger. The municipality also bought a brewery and converted the basement of the city hall into a gay rendezvous for wining and dining.

Parks, green areas, and woodlands were expanded, and outdoor beauties were better preserved—this was a phase of municipal "socialism" very close to the heart of Lueger—all told, more than three-quarters of the surface of Greater Vienna were either open space or forested. Facilities for outdoor recreation, swimming and boating especially, were substantially enlarged. During the ascendancy of the Christian Socialists, furthermore, nearly one hundred new schools, more pleasing architecturally in general than existing ones and with light and airy classrooms, were opened. Crèches for children of working mothers and resources for adult education multiplied. Government was managed with integrity, but criticism never ceased because the administration was not moving faster to transform Vienna into a "welfare city," and because of bureaucratic red tape in conducting business.

A pall of gloom settled over the Danubian capital in 1898 when it was learned that the Empress Elizabeth had been murdered. Disliking the pomp and stuffiness of court routine, this spirited Bavarian princess had gradually become estranged from the austere and punctilious Franz Josef and spent more and more time in study and travel. After the suicide of the Crown Prince Rudolph in 1889, melancholia gained steadily upon her. While in Swiss Geneva as the guest of Baroness Julie Rothschild, a Jewess of rare charm and culture, she was stabbed to death by an Italian anarchist. Following impressive funeral obsequies, witnessed by multitudes of mourning citizens, the Empress was interred in the Hapsburg family vault beneath the Capuchin Church; a crown of thorns, appropriately, was laid upon the sarcophagus.

Visits of foreign celebrities invariably excited the emotions of curious Viennese crowds. When Prince Bismarck, no longer the pilot of the German ship of state, arrived in the Hapsburg capital in 1892 to attend the wedding of his son, huge throngs extended him an enthusiastic welcome. The crowned heads of the three most powerful countries of Europe, Edward VII of Britain, William II of Germany, and Nicholas II of Russia, paid courtesy calls in 1903 on the Austrian monarch. The first two received cordial mass ovations, more exuberant in the case of the Briton than the German, but the reception given the Russian czar was restrained and frigid, partly because he entered and left the capital under tight security guard. Former President Theodore Roosevelt was warmly greeted by multitudes in 1910; he seems to have enjoyed rummaging about in secondhand bookshops at least as much as being entertained by the Emperor and prominent aristocrats.

Obscure men, who one day would stamp their personalities indelibly upon world history, learned to know the Hapsburg capital in the Lueger era or shortly afterward. Coming from a provincial Austrian town fifty miles away, Adolf Hitler lived in Vienna on three occasions, the last extending from 1908 to 1913. It is next to impossible to disentangle fact from fiction in the elaborate account of Hitler's Vienna years in his propagandistic autobiography, *Mein Kampf,* in which he describes Vienna as "the hardest, but also the most thorough, school of my life."

Painstaking research has disclosed, however, that Hitler actually invented the stories of the hardships he claimed he had experienced as a lowly laborer. From family sources his income was sufficient to get along slightly above the proletarian level for at least half of his stay in the Danubian metropolis. Yet he evidently lived beyond his means, though little or nothing was squandered on wine or women in neither of which Hitler took much interest. During part of the time he found shelter in a home for poor transients, obtaining some cash by the sale of insignificant pictures that he painted.

In all probability, Hitler would never have been anything more than a commonplace political agitator had he not picked up enduring convictions in Vienna. His intense nationalism, aversion to cosmopolitanism, contempt for the affluent middle classes and the proletarian masses, neurasthenic hatred of Marxian Socialism ("a pestilential whore") and Jewry ("a pestilence worse than the Black Death"), and detestation of parliamentary government— all these attitudes Hitler carried with him when in the spring of 1913 he emigrated to Bavarian Munich.

Conceivably while wandering about the capital, Hitler

passed Leon Trotsky on the street for he, too, made the city his home for several years. He fraternized with Victor Adler, who more than once assisted him with funds, and other Social Democratic chiefs. At Vienna, Trotsky published a Marxian paper *Pravda* (Truth), which was smuggled into the empire of the czars; highly personal views on Marxian policy and tactics that he set forth clashed irreconcilably with the opinions of other Russian revolutionary authors.

Early in 1913, Joseph Stalin arrived in the Hapsburg capital for a month long stay. His particular mission was to learn the thinking of Viennese Social Democrats on the tangled and complex nationality problems which beset the Hapsburg Monarchy and which might be useful in dealing with minorities if and when the Bolsheviks should capture control of Russia. When the First World War broke over Europe, Victor Adler assisted Trotsky in fleeing from Vienna; and he also interceded with Hapsburg authorities to secure the release of Lenin, who, on a visit to Austria, had been arrested at the beginning of the war as a czarist spy. If Trotsky and Lenin, the commanding personalities of the Bolshevik Revolution, had been interned in Austria throughout the war years, the stream of history would unquestionably have turned into different channels.

In March of 1910, Karl Lueger, afflicted for years with diabetes and failing eyesight, passed away. Apart from the many-sided changes in the texture of Vienna for which his administration was responsible, Lueger bequeathed to his beloved city a permanent legacy in the form of a vast increase in political consciousness among the masses—a bequest that redounded in time to the advantage of his Socialist adversaries. His tenure of the mayoralty constituted a sort of bridge between the laissez-faire ideology of the Liberals and the far-reaching welfare programs applied by the Social Democrats when they took command after the First World War. The Socialist administration, incidentally, authorized the erection on the Ring of a splendid bronze statue of the great Christian Socialist mayor.

ᵃᵍ 6 ᵍᵃ

Golden Kaiserstadt

Aᴏ the First World War, which shattered the Hapsburg Monarchy into fragments, it became fashionable in certain circles to look back to the "good, old days" of Vienna before the war wistfully and with nostalgia. Here was the capital—political, economic, and cultural—of a multinationality great power whose population exceeded fifty-one millions, and whose image of a "gay Vienna" had rooted itself in world folklore. It was defined in an aphorism of the Swiss man of letters, Gottfried Keller, as a "city of joy, of melody, that happy proud Vienna," an interpretation, it needs scarcely be repeated, that enshrined a large admixture of myth and legend.

Yet the Keller opinion was sustained by a rich diversity of cultural and intellectual talents, which indulged in experimentation to the point of turbulence. That climate has sometimes been regarded as clear evidence of a disillusioned and decadent Viennese intelligentsia. Certainly the general temper of the period, the rapid disintegration of Liberalism and the triumph of Christian Socialism, wrought powerfully upon interests and emphases of cultural workers.

A survey of cultural accomplishments may well begin with the world of music. Under the direction of Gustav

102

Mahler after 1897, the Vienna Opera reached the crest of its brilliance. An innovator and a perfectionist, Mahler enhanced the prestige of the pre-eminent artistic institution of central Europe, selecting the repertory to suit his own inclinations and bringing new singers to the fore. His domineering personality and caustic, tactless tongue raised up a pack of enemies, but he held on for a decade, then left for New York to direct the Metropolitan Opera Company and the Philharmonic Orchestra.

Composer as well as conductor, Mahler belonged in the mainstream of the Viennese classical tradition, though his music only slowly won acceptance by the major orchestras of the world. The spectacular *Eighth Symphony*, which is generally appraised as his masterpiece, is referred to as the *Symphony of a Thousand* because of the size of the orchestra and the large number of singers involved. The unfinished *Tenth Symphony* expresses calm resignation by the composer to the prospect of his impending death, due to a heart ailment.

Among the masters brought to the front by Mahler was the Berliner Bruno Walter (Schlesinger), who was appointed assistant director of the opera. Although a cosmopolitan, the interpretative musical style that Walter favored bore an unmistakable Viennese stamp. The successor of Mahler at the opera, Felix von Weingartner, a fiery-tempered son of Dalmatia, delighted in the productions of contemporary musicians, but criticisms grew so loud that he resigned after four years; he served several times as conductor in New York and Boston. To the storehouse of Vienna operas, Weingartner added *Orestes* and *Cain and Abel*, and he also composed notable symphonies and symphonic poems.

But the giant of creative music of the period was German-born Richard Strauss. His early (and short) symphonic poem, *Don Juan* (1888) evoked severe attack as extreme *avant garde*. His fortunes rose, however, with the opera *Elektra*, (1908) whose libretto was written by the foremost Viennese poet, Hugo von Hofmannsthal; thus began a remarkable collaboration that lasted a full generation. The music for *Elektra*, an adaptation of a gruesome Sophoclean drama of horror and murder, expressed intense emotions and achieved climaxes calculated to make the blood run faster, though the solo parts were exquisite in their delicacy and loveliness. Before the initial presentation of *Elektra* in Vienna, Hofmannsthal felt uneasy qualms about the reception, writing to Strauss, "the Vienna public of today is just as stubbornly opposed to everything new as in the days when *Fidelio* and *Don Giovanni* were voted failures."

In point of fact *Elektra* captivated contemporary critics far more than did Strauss' next creation, *The Rose Cavalier*, which later was acclaimed as a work of supreme genius. Superb craftsmanship and rare artistic beauty characterized the score of this diverting story of love and intrigue set in the reign of Maria Theresa. Gaiety combines with wistfulness in what is perhaps the most Viennese of operas when Sophie and Octavian counterpart a song of love to the lament of Marschallin for a bygone era. In *The Rose Cavalier*, as in other operas, Strauss gave fuller opportunities to the voices of women than was customary.

The composer himself thought his finest work was *The Woman Without Shadows*, a fairy tale opera in an Oriental environment. Rather original in conception and varied in artistic expression, it was written amidst the strains and stresses of the First World War. *Ariadne on Naxos*, which in a revised version had its Vienna première in 1916, was noted for exuberant love music and harlequinade. Unsurpassed in his prime for the pleasure he afforded listeners, Strauss continued to create great music for a generation following the war, but thereafter his powers declined and he suffered unmerited neglect.

Brilliant prima donnas contributed greatly to the eminence of Vienna in opera. Outstanding among the richly melodious stars were Selma Kurz, a protégée of Mahler, and the sopranos Marianne Brandt and Anna von Mildenburg (Bahr-Mildenburg), who did quite well as a Wagnerian heroine. For sheer versatility and sustained appeal on two continents, the Moravian-born diva Maria Jeritza belonged in a class apart. Beautiful to behold, she united a fresh and vital voice to exceptional acting talent. Those same qualities distinguished the tenor Leo Slezak. Richard Mayr, a bass of the first quality, starred in the operas of Strauss, and the baritone Erik Schmedes in Wagnerian dramas.

The heritage of Johann Strauss in operettas was carried forward by Franz Lehár, who came to Vienna from Hungary. His best known production, *The Merry Widow*, with its enchanting music and diverting text captivated Vienna and touched off a veritable craze in the United States. Even more fertile than Strauss, Lehár composed melodies for thirty operettas (*Count of Luxembourg* and *Gypsy Love*), which reinforced the international assumption that the Viennese way of life was as frivolous as it was jovial. That was true likewise of *The Dollar Princess* and *A Waltz Dream* by Leo Fall, and *The Chocolate Soldier*, whose libretto was based upon George B. Shaw's satirical *Arms and the Man*, by Oskar Straus.

To the playhouse resources of Vienna, the *Volksoper,* as it came to be known, was added in 1898. Until operas were presented as well as operettas, the new theater experienced box-office difficulties, in spite of the relative cheapness of the seats. Young, talented singers who performed acceptably at the *Volksoper* might be invited to appear at the Court Opera, as was the case with Maria Jeritza. The Vienna Concert Society, founded in 1900, enriched the world of music, especially after the opening (1913) of its Concert Hall, one room of which could seat 2,100 patrons. Celebrated pianists, like Ignace Paderewski and Sergei Rachmanninoff, repeatedly gave recitals to appreciative Viennese audiences.

The onetime Nestor of violinists in Vienna, Jacob M. Gruen, was eclipsed by the internationally renowned virtuoso Fritz Kreisler. For his brilliant technique and very personal interpretations, he was saluted as a "violinist's violinist." Warmly received as a teenage solo artist in the United States, Kreisler returned there after recovering from wounds sustained in the First World War. But the public mood after America became a belligerent obliged him as an Austrian to cancel recitals, and in seclusion he wrote a sprightly opera, *Apple Blossoms.* No musician of the postwar era was more beloved on both sides of the Atlantic than the courtly Kreisler.

A new chapter in the huge volume of musical pioneering in Vienna opened with the bold innovations of Arnold Schönberg. Though self-taught, in maturity he was recognized in Europe and America as an accomplished teacher and writer of musical theory. As a composer, he produced almost every type of music, writing rapidly and almost constantly. His principal early works, *Transfigured Night,* a string sextet in its original form, and a symphonic poem, *Pelléas and Mélisande*, attracted considerable attention, provoking quite as much ridicule as approval. The *Chamber Symphony*, designed for a small number of performers and complex in its orchestration, marked the end of the first phase of Schönberg's creativity. It was short, in contrast to the symphonies of his teacher, Mahler, which many listeners considered a boon.

To achieve freshness and originality in theme and harmony, Schönberg departed radically from conventional tonality. By reason of what is called twelve-tone atonality—a description that the composer personally disliked—his writing turned austere and cacophonous, repulsive to traditionalists. *Pierrot Lunaire*, a string of melodramatic pieces, to be recited rather than sung, grated on conservative Viennese ears, causing an explosive uproar when initially performed. To be appreciated, the works of Schönberg demanded more concentration than many musicgoers were willing to apply. On garrison duty in Vienna during the First World War, Schönberg found time to expand his serial technique of composition, which he developed to the full in the 1920's and after.

A spirit of revolt, encouraged by trends in France and by Japanese graphic art, pervaded Viennese painting after 1890. Breaking with academic artists, a group of younger painters—and architects—founded the Secession school (1897) and proceeded to place daringly different conceptions on canvas. "Each era its art," read the Secession motto, "each art its freedom." The men of the Secession not only exerted an important influence upon musicians and writers in Vienna, but made the Danubian capital known abroad for painting as it had never been known before.

They published *Vers sacrum,* an *avant garde* review, in which artistic problems were discussed without restraint, and they made a specialty of exhibiting the works of contemporary European artists in their curious headquarters in downtown Vienna.

For eight years Gustav Klimt presided over the Secession, then pulled away to form a rival school. His refined portraits of society ladies ("Frau Sonja Knips") made Klimt famous; he loved also to paint sensuous female nudes in suggestive poses, such as "Nuda Veritas"—the model, hair streaming across her shoulders, coyly admires herself in a mirror.

At his prime, the tastes of Klimt, spoken of as the *Jugendstil* or *l'art nouveau,* dominated Vienna painting. His bent for fantasy and rich coloration was displayed in paintings interpreting the several branches of knowledge prepared for the Aula of the University, but rejected by the University authorities. A representative specimen of Klimt's technique, "The Kiss," is an abstract mosaic with voluptuous contours and dazzling colors; by distorting the bodies the artist wished to depict the innermost feelings of the models. He gave an impetus to decorative artistry, applied from furniture to wallpaper, that lasted.

A second artistic rebel, Egon Schiele, originally inspired by Klimt, specialized in the delineation of the human anatomy. "The Family," for instance, shows three gaunt, grotesquely distorted naked figures, a father with fantastic hands, the big-bosomed mother, and a very solemn child, all with piercing eyes, suggestive of worry and anxiety. About 1910 Schiele developed a more distinctive style, and his inventiveness as a draftsman was well displayed in "Small Town"—each little house comes alive with its own smiling personality. He obviously enjoyed placing on canvas undernourished, sensuous girls of Vienna in postures that verged on the pornographic—in fact he was thrown into jail for paintings which the public authorities judged indecent. With almost Hogarthian ferocity, Hans Lorwin laid bare the privations, sodden pauperism, and wretchedness in the Danubian metropolis.

Klimt and the Dutchman Vincent van Gogh made a deep impression upon the many-sided Oskar Kokoschka. So did the psychoanalytical teachings of Sigmund Freud. As a portraitist, Kokoschka aimed at mirroring the states of mind of his subjects, as in paintings of his benefactor, the architect Adolf Loos, and of Karl Kraus, satirist; to interpret better what he thought he saw, Kokoschka chose cold and gloomy colors. As a student at the School of Arts and Crafts, he came under the fertile instruction of Berthold Loeffler, and showed unusual talent in designing decorative fans and cards. He also ventured into melodramatic playwriting (*The Burning Thornbush*), very difficult to comprehend. At the outset of the First World War, Kokoschka turned to painting grim realities, as seen in "The Knight Errant." After being wounded while fighting the Russians, he emigrated to Germany where his artistic style underwent a radical change; in London ultimately he took rank with the foremost painters of his period.

Sculptors in Vienna, in contrast to the esteemed painters, preferred conventional designs. Adding to his established reputation, Kaspar C. von Zumbusch carved notable equestrian statues of Field Marshal Radetzky and the Archduke Albert, victor over the Italians in 1866, which was placed on top of a fragment of the old city wall. For St. Stephen's, Edmund von Hellmer designed an interesting monument to commemorate the deliverance of Vienna from the Turks in 1683; he reached the peak of his powers in a majestic figure of Goethe seated in an armchair on the side of the Ringstrasse.

A professor at the Academy of Fine Arts, like Zumbusch and Hellmer, Hans Bitterlich chiseled a magnificent monument of the Empress Elizabeth in a sitting position for the *Volksgarten*. Deeply moved by this gift of the Austrian peoples, Emperor Franz Josef at the unveiling ceremonies predicted that "this monument will keep fresh in future generations the memory of the exalted Empress and Queen." It has. From the studio of Bitterlich also came a statue of Johann Gutenberg, called the father of printing, and several exquisite cemetery sculptures. Other workers in marble and bronze embellished public parks and squares with monuments to Strauss the Father and Lanner, early waltz masters, the architect Schmidt, the author Ludwig Anzengruber, Ferdinand Raimund, a popular nineteenth century playwright, the contemporary lyricist Nicholas Lenau, and the artist Hans Canon.

Structures designed by Otto Wagner inaugurated a period of original creativity in Viennese architecture. He placed emphasis upon the function a building was intended to serve and utilized new materials that technology had developed. His handsome Post Office Savings Bank accents lightness and simplicity together with novel applications of sculptured aluminum on the façade; the grand central hall, covered by a glass roof, admirably demonstrates Wagner's technical mastery. But his principal achievement, no doubt, is the chapel at Am Hof asylum, a large domed edifice of white marble, containing traces of baroque, but on the whole independent of traditional styles. Wagner was also responsible for several interesting residential blocks, adorned merely with a row of dark-blue tiles.

Wagner influenced Adolf Loos, who received his formal training in Germany, supplemented by a three year sojourn in the United States, where he acquired unmatched familiarity with American tastes in architecture. An exponent of "the new objectivity," Loos stressed functionalism and kept ornamentation at a minimum, as is seen, for instance, in a little Viennese tavern that he designed; planted in the stained-glass façade is a plain star-spangled banner, and smooth mahogany walls and mirrors extending to a ceiling of yellow marble are features of the interior. The only large structure created by Loos is a business establishment called Loos House (or Steiner House) on Michael Square. Seven stories tall, it is divided horizontally into two parts, the lower section, with classically detailed marble columns, leads into a pillared hall; the upper portion is devoid of decoration. Since Loos House stands directly across from the ornately elaborate entrance to the Hofburg, its puritanical simplicity is the more arresting.

The most passionately debated structure of the period was doubtless the home of the Secession in central Vienna, the work of Joseph M. Olbrich. The most conspicuous innovation is a gilded and pierced iron dome in the shape of a tree, which unsympathetic observers ridiculed as "a golden head of cabbage." Josef Hoffmann, who helped to decorate the Secession building, founded the world-renowned Vienna Workshops in which artistic metal goods, jewellry, glass tableware, and furniture were turned out with expert craftsmanship. Youths, moreover, were trained to design articles reflecting their artistic individuality or as interior decorators. One of them, Karl Witzmann, became internationally known for arranging exhibitions and as a designer of exquisite theatrical settings.

Viennese men of letters, writing after 1890, attracted an unprecedented readership at home and abroad. Themes and emphases responded to secular changes due to the progress of science and speculations thereon, intensifying urbanization and growth of the middle classes with their particular scale of values. Many an author, restless in mind, feeling a sense of hopeless pessimism exploited the morbid, even the macabre in the human personality. In perspective it was not difficult to detect resignation to the inescapable in much of the literary output of the period.

A "Young Vienna" clique gathered around Hermann Bahr, a writer with many facets, whose odd dress, patriarchal beard, and breezy flamboyance made him a man of distinction in the Danubian metropolis. Nightly "Young Vienna" converged on the Cafe Griensteidel to listen to the oracular utterances of Bahr and to exchange opinions on everything under the sun. Bahr's personal philosophy of culture passed under the name of "expressionism," by which he meant a studied effort to discover and expose the inner psychological states of individuals, not outward appearance. His voluminous writings in many forms possessed only limited value, though he attained international recognition for a comedy play, *The Concert*, a bizarre story of marital fidelity. Soon after fighting began in 1914, Bahr lampooned the martial spirit, but presently he was glorifying the high mission of the House of Hapsburg, and he who had been a Voltairean skeptic now lauded the Roman

Catholic Church as a bulwark of security for a storm-tossed generation (*The Voice*).

Not Bahr, but Arthur Schnitzler was the principal personality of "Young Vienna" and the sponsor of the so-called psychological school of imaginative Vienna authors. Whether in plays, novels, or short stories—many of them extensively translated—Schnitzler displayed such talent in analyzing human motives and in depicting mental aberrations that Freud saluted him as a "colleague." Skepticism and cynicism are recurrent emphases in Schnitzler's writing. For some critics he sang the swan song of hedonistic decadent Vienna, while others contend that his devotion to the timeless themes of love and death possess universal relevance. However that may be, his eminence reached such heights that the period is sometimes called "The Age of Schnitzler." Indicative of his enduring significance, the group of American literary scholars recently organized an International Schnitzler Research Association.

A fine stylist, he relished barbed dialogue and ironical wit. He usually chose Vienna or Austrian resort areas frequented by well-to-do Viennese as the setting of his productions and preferred professional and cultural workers as his characters. Trained for medicine, Schnitzler introduced over a score of physicians to his pages.

He first caused a stir in literary circles with *Anatol*, a set of vignettes centered on a Viennese philanderer whose sole interest in life is attractive women. He almost misses his wedding because the night before he engaged in a final amorous fling. So recently as 1961 a Broadway adaptation of *Anatol* appeared as a musical comedy, *The Gay Life*; it featured dancing girls, and since it was billed as representing "The essential character of Vienna," a merry waltz was incorporated. For literary grace, none of Schnitzler's writing surpasses *Liebelei* (Light-O'-Love), a tragicly dramatic portrayal of the eternal human triangle. *The Lonely Way* taught that men who declined to serve their society, choosing instead frivolous self-indulgence, led empty unrewarding lives.

Schnitzler dealt with high Viennese aristocrats in the comedy *Countess Mizzi*, a sophisticated satire on ethics and moral behavior. Up to a point, *Professor Bernhardi* has an autobiographical flavor. A Jewish physician, Bernhardi, refuses to allow a priest to administer the sacrament of extreme unction to a girl who thinks she has regained health, though in fact she is at death's door. The central theme, however, is the cleavage between medical ethics and religious dogma, for the doctor is condemned for denying the rites of the church. In this play Schnitzler, who had personally experienced the sling and arrows of Jew-baiters, touched on the Jewish question in Vienna—something he seldom did in his works. Suspicion, dislike, hatred, he seemed to say, were the common fate of minorities, and Zionism was no true way to salvation. During the First World War he kept busy with his pen, and some of his most penetrating and intellectually stimulating writing was published after 1918.

In some respects Karl Kraus was the most influential writer of prewar Vienna, an avowed foe of Bahr and his "Young Vienna" satellites. The son of a wealthy Jewish family from Bohemia and a born polemicist, Kraus at the age of twenty-five began to publish a little, red-covered magazine, *Die Fackel* (The Torch). On its pages he exposed with the fervor of an Old Testament prophet everything he disliked—corrupt journalism, sham, and hypocrisy in the cultural arts, municipal misgovernment, the evils of capitalism, the shortcomings of the well-to-do classes, and Zionism. Incapable of dullness, Kraus made himself a potent moral and ethical force in Viennese life and letters.

Pieces that he wrote while the war was on he expanded in a big, though incoherent, drama, *Die letzten Tage der Menschheit* (*The Last Days of Humanity*). Mordantly satirical, the work disclosed much on Vienna living and feeling during "the years when characters from an operetta played the tragedy of mankind," as Kraus wrote. Admirers likened him to Dean Jonathan Swift, and many a Viennese author of the postwar generation acknowledged an obligation to Karl Kraus.

The playwright, Karl Schönherr, stood apart from the authors already discussed. A physician in Vienna, though in origin a Tyrolese, he united uncompromising realism with imaginative fancy and earnestness with humor. His first large box-office success, *The Soil*, dramatized both the peasant custom that a father exercised absolute mastery over his household and Tyrolean love of the soil. In a second stage triumph, *Faith and Fatherland*, skillfully constructed, Schönherr preached the lesson of toleration. The scene is set in the Reformation era when Protestant countryfolk were commanded to forswear the new religious teaching or they would be expelled from their ancestral homes. Sturdily, they reply that they will make any sacrifice rather than renounce Luther's Bible, so they are ruthlessly driven away. To shore up morale in the war years, Schönherr composed *People in Need*, in colloquial dialect, recalling the heroic struggle of Tyrolese mountaineers in 1809 to break the stranglehold of Napoleonic troops.

Vienna theatergoers, it may be interpolated, welcomed

the erection of several new playhouses. One of them the Deutsches Volkstheater, a handsome white stone temple surrounded by pretty gardens, enlarged opportunities to see popular folk dramas, while the repertory of the new Raimund Theater embraced plays of that category and more serious, classical productions, competing in a way for patronage with the Court Theater. Two neighborhood theaters were built: the Neues Wiener Stadt Theater and the Johann Strauss, and modest showhouses in the Prater and on the Kahlenberg played to capacity audiences in the summer months.

To the lengthy roll of superb actors on the Vienna stage was added the name of Josef G. I. Kainz. Blessed with a marvelous voice, flawless diction, and immense vitality, Kainz after a hard struggle and varied experience (including a triumphant guest tour of the United States) attained his lifelong ambition to follow Mitterwurzer at the Court Theater. He played most brilliantly in *Hamlet* and other Shakespearean works, as Cyrano de Bergerac, and in interpretations of the heroes of the dramas by Grillparzer. Theatrical critics and poets alike sang the praises of the genial and beloved Kainz.

The finest of the tragediennes, Hedwig Bleibtreu, worthily upheld the traditions of Charlotte Wolter at the Court Theater. From first to last she performed some two hundred roles, being at her best in the classics, as Sappho or Medea, or in the productions of Schönherr. Western moviegoers of a later generation learned of the unsurpassed histrionic qualities of Bleibtreu through "The Third Man."

So well patronized were the theaters that the writer Stefan Zweig felt that Vienna was in the grip of "theatromania," but a potential competitor had emerged, appealing to more popular and less expensive tastes: the cinema. It was in 1896 that the first motion-picture house was opened—a small cellar room on the Kohlmarkt—and by 1912 ninety-seven cinemas were going concerns with seats for thirty-six thousand.

The presence of women on the list of distinguished Viennese authors testified in one form to the progress of feminism. Baroness Marie von Ebner-Eschenbach, who was educated and married in the Hapsburg capital and spent a portion of each year there, wrote short stories and novels that placed her among the most prominent fiction writers in the German language; she was the first woman to be rewarded with an honorary doctorate by the University of Vienna. While she described with realism and wit all classes of society, she excelled when depicting the aristocracy, her own set. Nowhere are the prepossessions, the interests, and the frailties of the Austrian patriciate more competently disclosed than on her pages.

In *Countess Muchi*, a sheaf of letters really, a young heiress naïvely reveals herself as an arch foe of learning and culture, and a good deal is explained about marital infidelity in the aristocratic class. *After Death* tells of an exemplary landlord, among the indolent and dissolute many, who has real affection for the good earth and the peasantry toiling on it.

Bertha von Suttner acquired a world-wide reputation by a sensational novel, *Lay Down Your Arms*, a moving tract teaching pacifism. Greatly disturbed by the European wars of her young womanhood, Suttner set out in her great novel the horrors and suffering of warfare and appealed for international understanding and co-operation. If costly competition in armaments and wars ceased, the way would be opened, she argued, to solve the overarching social problems of the day.

"Lay Down Your Arms" served as the motto of a general peace movement in which Suttner took part. To foster the international mind, she visited the United States several times, addressing over a hundred meetings on one trip. It appears that Suttner influenced the Swedish dynamite king Alfred B. Nobel to found the Peace Prize that bears his name; in any case, she was the first woman upon whom that coveted honor was bestowed. Later co-recipient of the Prize was Alfred H. Fried, collaborator with Suttner in the cause of international peace.

In the person of Hugo von Hofmannsthal, the Hapsburg capital possessed a poetic and literary genius of the first order, most generally remembered for his long and fruitful association with Richard Strauss as librettist. Like Schnitzler, with whom he fraternized in "Young Vienna" and later, Hofmannsthal was constantly preoccupied with the mystery of death, and he found inspiration and subject matter in the accomplishments of bygone centuries. To his way of thinking creative writers had a bounden duty to counteract the onrushing flood of materialism. He was firmly rooted in the soil of Vienna which he once described as "that big, small, heavy and light-winged town of flippant days and profound dreams, that town which it is easier to love and hate than to understand and leave."

At the age of seventeen Hofmannsthal excited enthusiasm in the Viennese intelligentsia with a sophisticated, lyrical drama in verse entitled *Gestern* (Yesterday). Written with a superb sense of vocabulary, it revealed a mind almost too hospitable to ideas and contained undertones of cynicism, world weariness, and melancholy. Goethe reborn, certain Viennese intellectuals called Hofmannsthal, which must have gratified the poet since he had chosen the greatest of German men of letters as his ideal.

The addiction of Hofmannsthal to art for art's sake, his desperate striving for perfection, and his profound concern for the past are abundantly illustrated in *The Death of Titian*. Another drama, *Death and the Fool*, expertly analyzes the apprehensions common to youth. At about twenty-five it looked as though Hofmannsthal had exhausted his capacity for artistic creativity. That, however, was only a passing mood, for, laying aside the creed of aestheticism, he composed the brilliant lyrics for *Elektra* and followed that up with the charming verse of *The Rose Cavalier*.

If there was any doubt that Hofmannsthal had abandoned the realm of art for art's sake, it was dispelled by a mystery play, *Jedermann* (Everyman). In the estimate of many literary critics he reached the summit of his intellectual powers in this tale of sin, repentance, and redemption, exalting the Christian virtues of tolerance and charity. Couched in language comprehensible to ordinary theatergoers and presented annually at Salzburg after 1918, *Jedermann* attained immense popularity.

Turning politician and propagandist while the First World War raged, Hofmannsthal penned essays extolling the mission of Austria (much as Bahr did) and seeking to foster an ardent patriotism. He prepared moving panegyrics on Prince Eugene of Savoy and Empress Maria Theresa and edited books glorifying the achievements of Austria. It was all in vain, and the destruction of the venerable Monarchy in 1918 left him paralyzed for a time.

Another member of the "Young Vienna" circle, Richard

Beer-Hofmann brought out a short, but exquisite poem, *Lullaby for Miriam,* hymning the loneliness of existence and the puzzles of life and the chaotic universe. His most respected play, *The Count of Charolais* was a good example of the products of the Vienna psychological school; human beings, it taught, are merely pawns on the chessboard of life pushed about by inscrutable fate. Becoming an impassioned Zionist, Beer-Hofmann composed allegorical dramas intended to promote the cause of a Jewish national home (*Jaákob's Dream*). His best writing was published after the First World War, as was true of a large part of the most prized work of Hofmannsthal and in lesser degree of Schnitzler.

The concerns of the Vienna proletariat had a compelling poetic voice in Alfons Petzhold, of German peasant stock. As a youth in Vienna he was frequently ill, wandered from job to job, and took up with Social Democracy, though the orthodox Marxist ideology meant less to him than prompt amelioration of the lot of industrial wage-earning households. *Tales from My Street,* masterly in depth of sentiment and in language, delineated in verse the harsh early manhood of Petzhold and stridently called for social fairness. Here as in *Ballads on Revolution,* he sharply castigated the state, the Roman Church, and the regime of private capitalism.

But upon the outbreak of the First World War, Petzhold published poetry that might equally well have been created by any bourgeois evangelist of victory. As the ghastly struggle lengthened out, though, his verse expressed detestation of the endless carnage and affection for men of all lands. Austrian authorities laid a ban on the circulation of these pacifist tracts for the times.

⋙ 7 ⋘

Science and Scholarship

THE UNIVERSITY OF VIENNA and the professional colleges and academies, nurseries of the intelligentsia, prospered after 1890. For instruction in commerce and soil culture splendidly equipped edifices were constructed. Scarcely a quarter century after the opening of the new University structure, it was discovered that it was too small. Seminars, clinics, research centers, such as a Physiological Institute (1898) and an Institute for Experimental Pharmacology, multiplied, and the University botanical garden was substantially extended for teaching purposes.

At the University teaching personnel increased to four times the number of 1850, and savants emphasized independent investigation as never before. By 1910, student enrollment approached the ten thousand mark, a 40 per cent growth in a little more than a decade. Women were admitted in 1897 to the philosophical faculty without reservations and three years later to the medical school, but the faculty of law held back until 1919. About two University students out of five matriculated in the law faculty, somewhat fewer in the philosophical departments, about one in four in medicine, and the rest in theology. So rapid was the increase of medical students that Viennese physicians, many of whom were hardly able to earn a decent living, applied pressure to restrict admissions. Something like 40 per cent of all students who entered the University managed to obtain the coveted doctorate.

The student body at the Technical College ranged beyond three thousand, a very considerable gain, and the smaller institutions for professional education likewise expanded. Owing in part to relatively high living costs in Vienna, foreign students were not numerous, except in medicine. Pan-German and anticlerical sympathies were strong in German-speaking student corps or fraternities, which engaged from time to time in rowdy affrays with Jews, Slavs, and Italians. Pitched battles were fought in 1907–08 between German and Italian students, both groups using cudgels, brass knuckles, and even revolvers; the Italians wanted an Italian section in the faculty of law at Vienna and an Italian-speaking University at Trieste. Police could not lawfully interfere so long as disorders were confined to the precincts of the University. During a sharp controversy with professors over municipal policy, Lueger tartly remarked that the learned gentlemen could employ themselves to better advantage by preventing explosive student eruptions.

Opportunities for adult education in Vienna were considerably enlarged. Of particular significance was the Urania, patterned on a Berlin model, which offered concerts and lectures of almost university quality on a broad range of subjects; its permanent home was dedicated in 1910, and branches were opened in the suburbs. Educated Social Democrats, like the University historian Ludo M. Hartmann, promoted programs of learning for wage earners, classes often meeting in gloomy cellars. Catholic and secular societies established new libraries and reading rooms, making books available to anyone who cared to read them.

Acts of the Austrian legislature placed the press less at the mercy of government officials, and the number of Viennese publications increased substantially, though many were too short-lived to have historical importance. A few, however, developed into important organs of opinion, as was the case with the *Reichspost*, the principal mouthpiece of clericalism. It was published by militant Roman Catholics, and being the recipient of subsidies from Church sources and the nobility, it eventually absorbed the *Vaterland*, traditional spokesman of church interests. Taking as its slogan "an independent paper for the Christian people of Austria," the *Reichspost* vigorously fought the Liberal press of Vienna (without equaling it in literary quality) and championed the cause of Christian Socialism. It indulged in a good deal of anti-Jewish agitation and matched Socialist papers in clamoring for extension of the franchise right; in domestic and foreign policies, it stood steadfastly for the interests of the Hapsburg crown. Issued twice daily, the *Reichspost* at its peak had a total circulation of about thirty-two thousand.

To the "Liberal" press was added *Die Zeit*, which frankly avowed that it intended to emulate a New York weekly, *The Nation*, and to rival the veteran *Neue Freie Presse*. Copy by the independently minded chief editor Heinrich Kanner contributed substantially to building up the prestige of *Die Zeit*, which, after it went over to daily publication (1902), was probably more widely read abroad than any Vienna newspaper except the *Neue Freie Presse*. Popular and learned writers prepared cultural articles, especially for the Sunday literary supplement.

A valuable recruit to the quality press was the leading Socialist newspaper, *Arbeiter Zeitung*, which became a daily in 1895, and its circulation climbed from twenty-four thousand (1900) to around fifty-four thousand (1914). Instead of revolutionary Marxism, editorial policy adhered to a moderate, gradualist interpretation of the creed; it had infinitely more to say about manhood suffrage, for instance, than about class warfare. Victor Adler and the longtime chief editor Friederich Austerlitz, a self-educated journalist with broad social and intellectual interests, stamped their personalities on the *Arbeiter Zeitung*, making it not only a powerful instrument for propagating Socialist news and views but a very useful repository of knowledge on basic social conditions in Vienna. To attract a larger readership, the cultural section of the paper was steadily toned up, in one way by serial publication of fiction by popular native and foreign novelists.

In a period of marvelous medical discoveries in Europe, Viennese investigators accomplished important work in nearly every department of the healing art. The favorite pupil of Billroth, Anton Eiselsberg, added new knowledge to operations on the stomach and neurosurgery, and he was an expert clinician. On a lecture tour to America he heightened the renown of the Vienna school in the United States. A surgeon at the front during the First World War, Eiselsberg also devised improved artificial limbs for wounded men.

The outstanding internist at Vienna, Carl W. H. Nothnagel, a Prussian by birth, was appointed (1882) professor of pathology and therapy after experience in several German universities. He rapidly acquired a great reputation by reason of discoveries on the action of the heart (ironically he died of heart disease), researches on the blood vessels, and remarkable skill as a diagnostician. Nothnagel's writings, such as *Special Pathology and Therapy*, made him internationally known, and patients were sent to him from all over the globe. As a physician, as a teacher, and as a man, Nothnagel was a savant of the highest type, setting a wonderful example for his students. His frequently repeated dictum that "only a good man can be a good doctor" was carved on the memorial to him in the University arcades.

Thousands of students heard the distinguished Viennese lecturer on the anatomy and pathology of the ear, Adam Politzer, and far more studied his classic *Textbook on the Treatment of Ear Ailments*, which was printed in many editions and was long unsurpassed anywhere. His method of treating diseases of the middle ear became so famous that the term "politzering" was incorporated in the vocabulary of medicine. In the prime of his career, Politzer treated as many as fifteen thousand patients annually, and he retained keen scientific interests (shown in a hundred original papers) down to his death at the patriarchal age of eighty-five.

The ablest student of Politzer, Robert Bárány, received the Nobel Prize in medicine for researches on the physiology and pathology of the vestibular apparatus of the ear. By devising simple methods of investigating the functions of the semicircular canals of the ear and of the cerebellum, Bárány smoothed the way to a reliable technique for the diagnosis of inflammation of the ear and kindred complaints. His book on these subjects attracted world-wide usage by specialists concerned with ear ailments, and

Bárány also contributed importantly to surgical treatment of the causes of progressive deafness in adults. Captured by the Russians in the First World War, he was freed through Swedish intervention, and spent the rest of his career at Upsala University in Sweden.

The international prestige of Vienna in ophthalmology was raised to higher levels by Emil Fuchs, whose treatise on *The Causes and Prevention of Blindness* and a textbook on the care and treatment of the eye were standard authorities on their subjects and were translated into the principal European and Oriental languages. Fuchs studied, described, and contrived alleviations for every form of eye ailment met with in Europe and investigated on the spot endemic diseases of the eye in all parts of the world. Fuchs prided himself on the dexterity and artistry with which he performed cataract and other operations on the eye, saving or restoring the sight of thousands. His clinic acquired the reputation of being the best in existence and attracted unusual cases from everywhere; if Fuchs could not cure an eye affliction, no one could, it was said. At the University, he pioneered in presenting lectures in the English language, primarily for American physicians, and he also lectured in the United States.

Moriz Kaposi, the heir of the celebrated dermatologist Hebra, studying skin diseases and syphilis from the standpoint of pathological anatomy, made several valuable discoveries. Through articles and books like *The Pathology and Therapy of Skin Diseases* and a *Handbook on Syphilis*, Kaposi achieved unexcelled authority among skin specialists. Exceptional research facilities and superb teachers, Anton Weichselbaum notably, enabled Vienna to maintain its international standing as a leading center for the study of pathological anatomy.

Original researches on diseases of children, the so-called Pirquet reaction method of inoculation, and studies on allergy placed Clemens von Pirquet among the best-known medical men of his generation. In the *New System of Feeding,* Pirquet disclosed new knowledge on the measurement of nutritive values and on the food requirements of children; applied during the First World War and in the troubled aftermath, that knowledge saved the lives of thousands of Viennese boys and girls. A large number of Americans studied with Pirquet in Vienna or heard him lecture at the Johns Hopkins and Minnesota universities.

Even better known in America, Adolf Lorenz, the most respected orthopedic surgeon of his generation, crossed the Atlantic a score of times. He specialized in the treatment of foot, hip, and spinal deformities, applying a technique of external manipulation. Bloodless, novel methods of surgery made Lorenz the subject of intense controversy, but he simply laughed at his detractors and went on relieving cases with results that almost verged on the miraculous.

The foundations of the world-wide repute of Vienna for the treatment of mental disorders were laid by Richard von Krafft-Ebing. His investigations and writing ranged over neurology, psychiatry, and criminality; *Sexual Psychopathy* was printed in a record number of editions. Still more distinguished was his successor Julius Wagner von Jauregg, whose discoveries would one day make him a Nobel laureate (1927). After finding ways of dealing with cretinism and related thyroid diseases, he searched for cures of mental illness by means of febrile infection. Year after year he patiently carried on experiments seeking to conquer progressive paralysis—an affliction that often led to imbecility and was presumed to be incurable. By inoculating patients suffering from paralysis with organisms that cause malaria, he succeeded in relieving a third of the cases. The fundamental principle of fever therapy was eventually applied to other types of illness.

Referred to sometimes as the father of psychotherapy, Josef Breuer, who spent his whole life in Vienna, is more widely known as a teacher of and subsequently a collaborator with Sigmund Freud. He loaned him money, sent patients to him, and they worked together on a catharsis method for treating hysteria, setting forth their findings in *Studies in Hysteria*. It was the conviction of Breuer that joint studies with Freud furnished the latter with the ground plan of psychoanalysis; in time, the two scientists became estranged, Breuer resenting the dogmatism and dynamism of Freud.

No Viennese in all of history has been so much talked about as Sigmund Freud—medical scientist and philosopher. In time the terms he employed—repressions, complexes, neuroses—insinuated themselves into everyday conversation. His theories affected the thinking and creativity of artists, novelists, philosophers of child education; and students of mythology, religion, and history acknowledged a debt to him. Excessive adulation of Freud, on the one hand, matched excessive hostility on the other. In any event, he will be remembered as a pioneer in psychoanalysis (a term he invented), which opened new avenues to understanding the hidden recesses of the human mind and to the treatment of the disturbed personality. In dedication to the advancement of knowledge, talent, and character Freud possessed the attributes of greatness.

Emigrating as a youth from Moravia to Vienna, Freud obtained a doctorate (1881) in medicine at the University and supplemented that with postgraduate study in Vienna and Paris. For several years he engaged in research in physiology and neuroanatomy before switching to his major lifework in clinical psychiatry. While struggling to gain a foothold in the medical profession in Vienna, he experienced the indignities of penury, and, as a Jew, he was exposed to humiliating outbursts of prejudice. "It is misery," he exclaimed, "to live here." Although proud of his Jewish heritage in its secular aspects, which he regarded as a goad to his accomplishments, Freud was not an observant Jew, for he thought all religions were infantile flights from reality. His atheistic outlook rested upon a materialistic conception of man and the world.

His magnum opus, *Interpretation of Dreams,* was published in 1900 and his second most important book, *Three Essays on the Theory of Sexuality,* five years later. According to Freud, far the largest area of the human mind is the unconscious, in which are tucked away all the experiences of an individual from birth; the conscious zone is comparatively narrow. The dynamic elements in mental processes, Freud decided, are repressed urges and drives in the unconscious area. If these desires, usually of a sexual character, in the broad meaning of the term, are not appeased, grave mental disorders result. By means of the therapy of psychoanalysis, a sufferer might be able to free himself from complexes and neuroses and sublimate natural impulses in healthy, purposeful activity.

129

The doctrines of Freud provoked a flood of jeers and castigation from Viennese specialists on mental illness. Partisans of a collectivist pattern of society, moreover, condemned the Freudian preoccupation with the individual and the stress laid upon the biological factors in behavior; according to the eminent Hungarian Marxist critic, George Lukács, Freud belongs "to the intellectual disasters of the imperialist period." Still other critics assailed the Freudian theories on the score that they justified unrestrained libertinism, which would wreck the inherited morality. But an invitation to lecture at Clark University, Worcester, Massachusetts, in 1909 advertised that Freud had become an international personality.

At Vienna heretical schisms developed inside the small band of Freud's students. Dissenters engaged in academic polemics with all the fierceness of zealots. One group, Carl G. Jung in the vanguard, contended that religious belief possessed therapeutic value for certain disturbed personalities and that Freud attached too much weight to sexuality. A second set of insurgents, best personified by Alfred Adler, concluded that inferiority complexes more adequately accounted for neuroses than sexual inhibitions. Be that as it may, Freudian ideas, diluted or otherwise, penetrated deeply into the scientific and popular thought of the twentieth century.

Several Viennese scientists and scholars, other than medical specialists, attained international stature. Consider, for instance, Julius Hann, universally respected for research in climatology and meteorology. His masterpiece, *A Handbook of Climatology*, which in its final version was issued in three stately volumes, is an invaluable work, a compilation of what was known about climate all over the globe. In an orderly and systematic fashion and with unusual vividness, Hann explained the bearing of climate upon harvests and human energy and presented a wealth of detailed and exact information about temperature, rainfall, and the like. A companion *Handbook of Meteorology* was likewise indispensable for experts in its branch of knowledge.

On the basis of materials gathered on extensive travels, Friedrich K. A. Penck prepared books on geography and geology that earned him world-wide renown. He was esteemed especially for works on glaciers and moraines in the Alpine region—*The Alps in the Ice Age*—classification of land forms—*The Morphology of the Earth's Surface*—and for the advancement of regional geography. A second indefatigable traveler, Richard Wettstein, collected botanical specimens and made scientific observations in the tropics and the Near East which considerably enriched knowledge. An astute administrator, he also succeeded in getting the old University botanical gardens enlarged.

If one historian were to be selected to personify the refined methods of investigation, thoroughness, and carefulness that were practiced in Vienna, he would be Oswald Redlich. Primarily, his interest lay in the Middle Ages, particularly in the early Hapsburgs on which he edited a vast quantity of original documents. His big biography of *Rudolf of Hapsburg* (1903), solidly grounded on critical scrutiny of every scrap of pertinent evidence and written with elegance, placed Redlich at the top of Viennese historical scholarship. A tireless researcher, he kept writing scholarly monographs into the ninth decade of his life.

Less keen perhaps, less painstakingly accurate than

Redlich, but his superior in breadth of interest, Alphons Dopsch won recognition by an original *Social and Economic History of the Alpine Slavs* and followed that up with the *Economic Development in the Carolingian Era.* Learned articles, on special topics or by way of reply to critics, consolidated the prestige of Dopsch among professional scholars. Ludo M. Hartmann composed a *History of Italy in the Middle Ages*; though unfinished at the time of his death, this work illuminated Italian economic and social developments and learnedly demonstrated the importance of medieval Italy for German-speaking Europe. His scrupulous scholarship was reinforced by a powerful imagination, and he brought to his writing both original ideas about the past and involvement with contemporary social problems. With a band of collaborators, Hartmann prepared a large history of mankind, which was intended to popularize knowledge about the past, an enterprise that was in keeping with the activity of Hartmann as a promoter of adult education.

Historical knowledge of the Balkan Slavs, as well as the ethnography and the geography of the Balkan area, was wonderfully enlarged by Josef K. Jireček, a Viennese of Czech parentage. At the age of twenty-one he caused a publishing sensation by a *History of the Bulgars*, which was widely translated and has never been wholly superseded. But his major contribution was a *History of the Serbs* for which he studied archival materials hitherto neglected by investigators. His University seminar on the history of eastern Europe held front rank among institutions of its kind. A fascinating lecturer, who drew crowds of students as well as curious citizens to his lecture hall, August Fournier made his mark with a multivolumned and stylistically attractive biography of Napoleon, which remains a standard work.

Busy though he was as a publicist and for several years as a Vienna city councilman, Heinrich Friedjung composed a reliable history of *The Struggle for Supremacy in Germany*, describing the rivalry of the 1850's and 1860's between Austria and Prussia. A monumental *Age of Imperialism*, by Friedjung, which comprehensively surveyed the recent past of Europe, was interrupted by his death; the finishing touches were applied by Alfred F. Pribram, who together with a second younger scholar interested in diplomatic and economic affairs, Heinrich von Srbik, would produce histories of high distinction after 1918.

In his later Vienna period, Ernst Mach, an eminent physicist, concentrated his immense intellectual powers on philosophy and ethics for the most part. *The Science of Mechanics* exhibited remarkable talent for writing the history of the complicated discipline of mechanics, and in *Contributions to the Analysis of Sensations*, Mach exposed systematically a philosophy of materialism and agnosticism. The American, William James, alluded to the "wonderful originality" of his friend's work. A tough-minded, unassuming savant, Mach adhered to positivism, that is, the strong tendency to rely exclusively upon the facts of objective experience and to eschew metaphysical and supernatural speculations. He preferred to describe rather than to explain phenomena, and contended that knowledge possessed value only insofar as it facilitated modifications in the material and social environment.

A personal pattern of ethics hammered out by Mach emphasized application of democratic principles, more equitable distribution of wealth, and the importance of unflagging campaigns against ignorance and inhumanities. This creed, which encouraged skepticism when not atheism, Mach diffused in learned literature, from a University chair, and through lectures for popular consumption. By indirection, he prepared the way for a school of philosophical inquiry that rose to world fame after 1918—the Vienna circle of logical positivists.

Extensively read in the original German and in translations was a spacious survey of *Greek Thinkers* by Theodor Gomperz, which carried the story of Greek philosophy through Aristotle. Like many another Viennese intellectual, Gomperz was strongly attracted to the liberal views of John Stuart Mill, with whom he was well acquainted, and whose writing on logic he put into German, adding an interpretative commentary. Besides remarkable talent as a linguist, the interest of Gomperz in the things of the mind and the spirit were protean; his lectures were among the most exciting delivered at the University, and his hospitable home was a noted intellectual rendezvous.

Economists in the University faculty of jurisprudence perpetuated and enlarged upon the teachings of the "Austrian School." Eugen von Philippovich, a disciple of Karl Menger on methods of investigation and basic principles, published the principal textbook of the Vienna economists, *Fundamentals of Political Economy*, and a more mature work, *The Development of Economic Ideas in the Nineteenth Century*. He displayed, too, a lifelong interest in social reform based upon sound theoretical foundations, and exerted considerable influence upon Austrian social welfare legislation. A very careful investigation of the housing situation in Vienna by Philippovich, to which reference has previously been made, revealed shocking conditions, and is permanently valuable as an historical document. Americans who studied in Vienna and Viennese economists who emigrated to the United States carried the theories of the "Austrian School" across the Atlantic. After the group in Vienna had virtually disintegrated, one *émigré*, Joseph A. Schumpeter, planted its fundamental concepts at Harvard, and the better known Frederick A. Hayek, performed similarly at Chicago; his book, *The Road to Serfdom* would one day enjoy a large audience in America.

This chapter may properly be ended with a survey of Roman Catholicism in Vienna in the closing stage of Hapsburg history. Science, scholarship, and secularism encouraged indifference to religion in the middle classes, while Social Democracy, this-worldly and agnostic, confronted the Church with a formidable opponent. Certain priests warned that hell-fire punishment awaited individuals who embraced Socialism, and, in turn, Socialist spokesmen taught that Roman Catholicism was the unsleeping enemy of the proletariat.

And the Pan-German agitation of George von Schoenerer, appreciating that the Roman Catholic Church was a big obstacle to union with imperial Germany, carried on an "Emancipation from Rome" (*Los von Rom*) campaign. Turning Protestant himself, Schoenerer exhorted, "Let us break the chains which tie us to a church hostile to Germanism." In spite of vigorous propaganda, partly financed by Protestants of Germany, secessions from Catholicism were not significant outside of student circles.

Catholicism in Vienna (and elsewhere) in the 1890's faced a challenge from "modernism," a liberal current among intellectuals intended to bring the Church into line with prevalent trends in science and scholarship. The foremost Viennese exemplar of "modernism," Albert J. M. Ehrhard, a learned church historian at the University, disclosed his convictions in works such as *Catholicism and the Twentieth Century*, which unloosed an impassioned uproar in clerical ranks. Ehrhard was obliged to resign from the faculty.

A second outcropping of "modernism" involved Ludwig Wahrmund, professor of church law at Innsbruck University and well-known as a foe of the clerical spirit. In a pamphlet on *The Catholic Attitude and Free Learning*, he reasoned that an unbridgeable chasm yawned between church orthodoxy and the findings of contemporary scholarship. Branded a "modernist" by infuriated churchmen, Wahrmund under pressure relinquished his professorship, and the offensive brochure was suppressed. But anticlerical students in Vienna rallied to the support of Wahrmund and, egged on by the "liberal" press, threatened to boycott the University unless the professor was restored to his chair. Tempers cooled down, however, when Austrian authorities transferred Wahrmund to Prague University and published solemn assurances that academic freedom would not again be infringed. Clerically minded men inveighed heatedly against the University, Mayor Lueger reviling the institution as a "hotbed of subversive ideas, revolution, godlessness and antipatriotism."

A Vatican encyclical of 1907—*Pascendi Dominici regis*—condemned "modernism" as "the synthesis of all heresies," and extremely perilous for the Catholic creed. At most, "modernism" had only limited acceptance by the Vienna intelligentsia, and after the papal condemnation adherents were either silenced or they withdrew from the Church.

Despite the challenges from a variety of quarters, multitudes of Viennese held firmly to the faith of the fathers, though public observance was likely to be, as traditionally it had been, "a leisurely religion without fervor." Catholic agencies fought hard to protect and advance church interests. To aid and abet the Catholic press, the *Piusverein* installed boxes in churches in which contributions might be dropped. In spite of all the help rendered to the *Reichspost* and smaller clerical voices, it is probable that Roman Catholic journalism carried less weight in molding public sentiment in Vienna than it had in the 1870's.

The mightiest bulwark of the Church, however, was the Christian Socialist party, around which young priests particularly rallied. On the other hand, the head of Viennese Catholicism, Anton J. Cardinal Gruschka, like Cardinal Ganglbauer before him, disliked the Lueger movement, because of its economic program, and its anti-Jewish demagoguery. As a parish priest, Gruschka had fostered benevolent societies of Catholic journeymen, and as a cardinal he continued that activity, as well as combating deviations from Catholic orthodoxy; he also sponsored the erection of a number of suburban churches.

For many Viennese Catholics the Christian cross and the black and yellow emblems of the House of Hapsburg were sacred, intertwined symbols. Hierarchy and clergy proclaimed unceasingly that prevailing governmental institutions possessed the sanction of the Almighty and therefore were to be cherished, respected, and obeyed. Churchmen also resisted the schismatic Old Catholics, who only slowly enlarged their membership, and they forced the people called Methodists, regarded as a dangerous menace to Catholicism, to abandon their chapel; the pastor was forbidden to preach anywhere in the Danubian metropolis.

Francis K. Nagl, chosen archbishop in 1911 and later named a cardinal, openly sympathized with the objectives and spirit of Christian Socialism, by then a declining force in Vienna life. He had ultimate responsibility for arranging a great Eucharistic Congress (1912), which manifested the strength and vitality of Viennese Catholicism. The papal representative at the gathering, Dutch Cardinal Willem M. van Rossum, was welcomed with enthusiastic popular ovations, as though he were in fact the Pope himself. At the opening ceremonies of the Congress in the huge rotunda at the Prater, scores of members of the Hapsburg family attended together with tens of thousands of ordinary Viennese and visitors who flocked into the capital.

The most impressive spectacle, though, was an enormous parade to an outdoor Mass. Aristocrats on horseback led the procession followed by a long retinue of carriages containing high dignitaries of Church and state, and carriages of archducal couples drawn by milk-white Lippizaner horses from the imperial stud. Cardinals van Rossum and Nagl rode in the glittering Hapsburg coronation coach, holding the Host aloft. Escorted by cavalrymen, the Emperor Franz Josef appeared in the uniform of a field marshal; he obediently opened and closed the door of the equipage of the papal legate and, with head uncovered, ostentatiously knelt in prayer in a public square. Banks of wet, shivering, parade-loving spectators lined the route of the procession, which required five hours to pass. The Congress quickened Catholic self-confidence and afforded the Viennese a pageant such as would not soon be witnessed again.

The Hapsburg Monarchy entered the First World War with Cardinal Friederick G. Piffl in the office of archbishop of Vienna. He felt that the Viennese burghers were too absorbed in the pursuit of pleasure for their own good and that moral decay, materialism, and eccentric cults were more alarming than housing congestion or material distress in the industrial wards. Shortly before the onset of the First World War, he united with fellow Austrian prelates in issuing a pastoral letter admonishing believers to resist the increasing passion for diversion. "Luxury, extravagance, and the search for pleasure," the document read, "are every day attaining greater dimensions and are a serious menace to the well being of the individual and the family. An insatiable desire for ostentation has become a disease which is eating at the root of the race. Dances and other forms of amusement aim not at beneficial relaxation, but at the excitement of the senses, while the majority of theatrical and other performances . . . disseminate immoral principles and glorify the most reprehensible acts."

Over against that ecclesiastical appraisal may fairly be set the thoughtful reflections of the novelist Stefan Zweig, who in *The World of Yesterday* comments on prewar Vienna. "At night the dim street lights of former times were replaced by electric lights," Zweig wrote, "the shops spread their tempting glow from the main streets out to the city limits. Thanks to the telephone one could talk at a distance from person to person. People moved about in horseless carriages with a new rapidity; they soared aloft, and the dream of Icarus was fulfilled.

"Comfort made its way from the houses of the fashionable to those of the middle class. It was no longer necessary to fetch water from the pump or the hallway, or to take the trouble to build a fire in the fireplace. Hygiene spread and filth disappeared. People became handsomer, stronger, healthier, as sport steeled their bodies. Fewer cripples and maimed and persons with goiters were seen on the streets.

"Progress was also made in social matters; year after year new rights were accorded to the individual, justice was administered more benignly and humanely, and even the problem of problems, the poverty of the great masses, no longer seemed insurmountable. The right to vote was being accorded to wider circles, and with it the possibility of legally protecting their interests. Sociologists and professors competed with one another to create healthier and happier living conditions for the proletariat.

"There was as little belief in the possibility of such barbaric declines as wars between the peoples of Europe as there was in witches and ghosts. Our fathers were comfortably saturated with confidence in the unfailing and binding power of tolerance and conciliation. They honestly believed that the divergencies and the boundaries between nations and sects would gradually melt away into a common humanity.

"Hospitable and endowed with a particular talent for receptivity, the City [Vienna] drew the most diverse forces to it, loosened, propitiated, and pacified them. It was sweet to live here, in this atmosphere of spiritual conciliation, and subconsciously every citizen became supernational, cosmopolitan, a citizen of the world."

Tinged though the Zweig assessment was with nostalgia and not devoid of naïveté, it summarized, doubtless, the outlook of many an enlightened Viennese bourgeois as Europe moved toward the abyss of general conflict.

~§ 8 §~

Into the Abyss

T HE PASSING of Mayor Karl Lueger in 1910 left a big gap in the Vienna scene—not least in the administration of the municipality. Any man would have found it extremely difficult to try to fill his place, even though his Christian Socialists commanded nearly a five to one majority in the city council. In a political testament Lueger begged his party to carry forward the work he had sponsored and recommended an ardent Christian Socialist, Dr. Richard Weiskirchner, as his successor. But the nominee preferred to remain at his post in the Austrian ministry; however, when Weiskirchner was dropped as minister in 1912, he accepted the mayoralty robes and wore them into 1919.

The veteran Prince Alois Liechtenstein served as the titular head of the Christian Socialists. Factional rivalries gravely weakened the party at the very time that the militant Social Democrats were surging upward. At elections in 1911 for the Austrian parliament, Socialist candidates in Vienna won more than two-fifths of the votes, and their party would have captured the municipal council in all probability if the First World War had not intervened, forcing the postponement of elections.

As the almost immediate sequel to the 1911 balloting for

the imperial legislature, ominous proletarian convulsions rocked the Hapsburg capital. During a monster rally in front of the city hall in protest against rising costs of living and housing shortages, demonstrators chorused, "We want bread," "Away with capitalism," "Hurrah for the revolution." Vandalism, such as the destruction of streets cars, raced across the proletarian suburbs, and barricades were thrown up; street fighting with imperial troops ensued, resulting in two deaths at least. Disorderly citizens in the hundreds were arrested, and a threat to impose martial law in order to restore peace was published. Because it described the troubles as "A demonstration of despair," the *Arbeiter Zeitung* was confiscated.

While dark clouds of international conflict were steadily lowering over the horizon of Europe, Vienna was recurrently alarmed by an epidemic of espionage cases. The most sensational affair implicated Alfred Redl, director of the Hapsburg military secret service. It was discovered that Redl, hard-pressed for cash to appease his sexual appetite, had sold vital army information to agents of the Russian czar. Two fellow officers waited upon the culprit, laid the evidence before him, and placed a revolver on his table; trapped, Redl obeyed the etiquette of his profession by shooting himself. That episode and similar affairs only less scandalous aggravated worries in Vienna about the capacity of the Hapsburg state to fight, if war came.

Under circumstances that lie beyond the scope of this book, in July of 1914, Austria-Hungary became involved in the great European war. Just before the actual outbreak of fighting, a frenzied mass psychosis gripped Vienna, except for a small band of strait-laced, international Marxists. It was popularly imagined that the laurels of military victory would be plucked in a matter of months. But the mood of the capital changed when grim statistics on captured soldiers and on deaths in the armed forces poured in and tens of thousands of refugees swept into the city from the war zones. Trainloads of wounded and sick soldiers overwhelmed the hospitals, necessitating the conversion of public buildings and palaces of the aristocracy into medical centers. Families of men who were called to the colors had to be provided with the necessities of life.

Apparently, the Viennese satirist, Karl Kraus, coined the apothegm that in Berlin conditions were serious but not hopeless, while in Vienna conditions were hopeless but not serious. If ever accurate, which may be doubted, that piece of cynicism lost its validity in the war era. On the outskirts of the capital, hastily thrown up breastworks, laced with barbed wire, were constant reminders of the peril of Cossack invasion. In the Prater and elsewhere, open areas were converted into army training grounds, and factories concentrated heavily on making goods required to prosecute the fighting. Becoming propagandists, churchmen, university scholars, and literary men worked to sustain popular faith in the righteousness of the cause in hand, to intensify mass loathing of czarist Russia and perfidious Italy, and to strengthen confidence in ultimate victory.

The city council granted exceptional emergency powers to Mayor Weiskirchner, and it was not convened during the first eighteen months of the fighting. He consulted, however, with the *Stadtrat* and party chiefs on major municipal problems, and earned general respect for the honesty and impartiality with which perplexing questions like rationing of food and other necessities were handled and for campaigns against profiteering and epidemic disease. Experienced and capable administrator that he was, Weiskirchner directed city-wide drives to collect clothing, medical supplies, and metals desperately needed by the armed forces. Newspapers ran campaigns to obtain funds for various kinds of war relief, and women bent themselves sacrificially to tasks connected with the war effort.

After momentary hesitation in the summer of 1914, Vienna theaters and music halls resumed operations on nearly a peacetime scale, playing to capacity audiences, and cinemas supplemented the press in acquainting the public with the harsh realities of warfare. Blank spaces in newspapers testified to the rigorous character of the censorship, which evoked hot and endless protestations from editors— the *Arbeiter Zeitung* more boldly than the bourgeois press.

Viennese morale underwent ups and downs in response to what was known about the course of the war; but gathering privations impaired the will to fight through to victory. The longer the ordeal raged, the more desperate grew shortages of food, fuel, and everyday necessities. The wheat content of bread was cut down progressively and other commodities, even if rationed, were ever harder to secure. Unpalatable substitutes for coffee, so pleasant a part of Viennese living, and inadequate supplies of beer and wine and their costliness gnawed away at the martial spirit. Totally disregarding regulations, enterprising Viennese streamed into the countryside and traded their possessions with peasants for provisions; black marketeers amassed fortunes. On an over-all view, the purchasing power of wages of workers dwindled. The harder the struggle to survive and the longer the lists of imprisoned, wounded, and dead on the battlefronts, the deeper war weariness became.

Small-scale food riots in 1915 preceded massive demonstrations of famished Viennese in the following year. Beyond that, morale was depressed in the autumn of 1916 by the murder of the Austrian Premier Count Karl Stuergkh, while he was lunching in a downtown Vienna hotel. For the politically articulate, he personified both the suspension of ordinary civil liberties and the conduct of state business without benefit of parliament. The killer, Friedrich Adler, son of Victor and an unflinching adherent of the international tenet of Marxism, shouted as he fired, "Down with absolutism!" "We want peace." Responsible Socialist spokesmen disavowed any responsibility for the assassination of the prime minister, which Franz Josef thought a worse disaster than the loss of a battle.

On November 21, 1916, the Emperor, who had passed the eighty-sixth milestone, breathed his last. Despite his age he had kept toiling away on public matters throughout the war years. After the early phases of the conflict he seems to have harbored no illusions about the eventual outcome. His heart was deeply touched by Viennese manifestations of affection, and he was cut to the quick by the suffering and misery of his peoples.

For six days the body of the Emperor lay in state at Schönbrunn, then it rested three days more in the chapel of the Hofburg before conveyance to St. Stephen's for final consecration. Hour after hour church bells tolled a melancholy lament, and immense crowds watched the funeral procession passing from place to place. The deposit of the coffin of Franz Josef in the subterranean crypt of the Capuchin fathers vividly symbolized the end of an era for Vienna.

For Further Reading

FOR THE FRAMEWORK in which the Vienna of Franz Josef evolved, consult Arthur J. May, *The Hapsburg Monarchy, 1867–1914* (new ed., Cambridge, Mass., 1965) and *The Passing of the Hapsburg Monarchy* (Philadelphia, 1966). The standard account of the upheavals of 1848 is *The Vienna Revolution of 1848* (Austin, 1957) by R. John Rath.

GENERAL WORKS: William A. Jenks, *Vienna and the Young Hitler* (New York, 1960), excellent; Bruno Grimschitz and Erwin Mayer, *Vienna* (Vienna, 1951), comprehensive; Henry D. Sedgwick, *Vienna* (Indianapolis, 1938), light and entertaining; Jabez A. Mahan, *Vienna of Yesterday and Today* (Vienna, 1928), thin; Anna Eisenmenger, *Blockade* (New York, 1932), a graphic account of Vienna during the First World War.

ON JEWRY: Max Grunwald, *History of the Jews in Vienna* (Philadelphia, 1936), badly organized; Peter G. J. Pulzer, *The Rise of Political Anti-Semitism in Germany and Austria* (New York, 1964), competent; Alex Bein, *Theodore Herzl* (new ed., London, 1957), very good; Egon C. Corti, *The Reign of the House of Rothschild* (New York, 1928).

ON MEDICAL HISTORY: Adolf Lorenz, *My Life and Work* (New York, 1936); Ernest Jones, *The Life and Work of*

For Further Reading

Sigmund Freud (3 vols., New York, 1953–57), definitive; Thomas N. Bonner, *American Doctors and German Universities* (Lincoln, 1963), a quality production.

For an understanding of the philosopher Franz C. Brentano and his followers, see Howard O. Eaton, *The Austrian Philosophy of Values* (Norman, 1930). The best accounts in English of the "Austrian School" of economists are in Henry W. Spiegel, ed., *The Development of Economic Thought* (New York, 1952) and Joseph Schumpeter, *Ten Great Economists* (New York, 1951).

MUSIC: Max Graf, *The Legend of a Musical City* (New York, 1945), chatty; Henry Pleasants, ed., *Vienna's Golden Years of Music* (New York, 1950), on Eduard Hanslick; Patrick C. Hughes, *Great Opera Houses* (London, 1956); Richard Specht, *Johannes Brahms* (New York, 1930); Werner Wolff, *Anton Bruckner* (New York, 1942); Frank Walker, *Hugo Wolf* (London, 1951); Ada B. Teetgen, *The Waltz Kings of Old Vienna* (New York, 1940); Heinrich E. Jacob, *Johann Strauss, Father and Son* (New York, 1940); Bruno Walter, *Gustav Mahler* (New York, 1941); William Mann, *Richard Strauss* (London, 1964), excellent; Louis P. Lochner, *Fritz Kreisler* (New York, 1950); Maria Jeritza, *Sunlight and Song* (New York, 1924), autobiographical; Hans H. Stuckenschmidt, *Arnold Schoenberg* (London, 1959); Duka Newlin, *Bruckner, Mahler, Schoenberg* (New York, 1947), technical.

PAINTING: David C. Preyer, *The Art of the Vienna Galleries* (new ed., Boston, 1926); Edith Hofmann, *Kokoschka* (London, 1947), vivid.

LITERATURE: Douglas Yates, *Franz Grillparzer* (Oxford, 1946), analytical; Edna Purdie, *Friedrich Hebbel* (London, 1932); M. Macken, *Hermann Bahr* (Dublin, 1926); Solo-

147

mon Liptzin, *Arthur Schnitzler* (New York, 1932) and *Richard Beer-Hofmann* (New York, 1936); Erich Heller, *The Disinherited Mind* (new ed., Cambridge, England, 1962), has an essay on Karl Kraus; Brian Coughlin, *Hofmannsthal's Festival Dramas* (Cambridge, England, 1964), with extensive bibliographies; Gerhard Masur, *Prophets of Yesterday* (New York, 1961), compact appreciations of Hofmannsthal and Freud.

Gustav Gugitz, ed., *Bibliographie zur Geschichte und Stadtkunde von Wien* (5 vols., 1947–62), slight gaps, otherwise exhaustive; Anton Bettelheim, et al., eds., *Neue Oesterreichische Biographie* and continued as *Grosse Oesterreicher* (1925——).

GENERAL WORKS: Karl Ziak, ed., *Unvergaenliches Wien* (Vienna, 1963), by a team of specialists; Hans Tietze, *Wien* (Vienna, 1931), the best one volume work; Heinrich Srbik and Reinhold Lorenz, *Die Geschichtliche Stellung Wiens, 1740–1918* (Vienna, 1962); Rudolf Till, *Geschichte der Wiener Stadtverwaltung* (Vienna, 1957) and *Wiens Geschichtliche Stellung* (Vienna, 1947); Friedrich Walter, *Wien* (3 vols., Vienna, 1940–44), marred by the Nazi environment in which it was written; Reinhard E. Petermann, *Wien* (new ed., Vienna, 1913); Richard Kralik, *Geschichte der Stadt Wien* (new ed., Vienna, 1926), a chronicle; Ann T. Leitich, *Damals in Wien* (Vienna, 1952).

SPECIAL TOPICS: Felix Czeike, *Liberale, Christlichsoziale, und Sozialdemokratische Kommunalpolitik* (Vienna, 1962); Johann C. Allmayer-Beck, *Vogelsang* (Vienna, 1952); Kurt Skalnik, *Karl Lueger* (Vienna, 1954); Max Ermers, *Victor Adler* (Vienna, 1932); Lorenz Reinhold, *Die Wiener Ringstrasse* (new ed., Vienna, 1944); Hans Pemmer, *Der Wiener Prater* (Vienna, 1935); Gustav Gugitz,

Das Wiener Kaffeehaus (Vienna, 1943), delightful; Ann T. Leitich, *Die Wienerin* (Stuttgart, 1939); Richard Meister, *Geschichte der Wiener Universitaet* (Vienna, 1934), comprehensive; Leopold Schoenbauer, *Das Medizinische Wien* (new ed., Vienna, 1947); Max Neuberger, *Das Allgemeine Krankenhaus* (Vienna, 1935); Robert Gersuny, *Theodor Billroth* (Vienna, 1922), brief; Max Neuberger, *Hermann Nothnagel* (Vienna, 1922); H. Montane, *Die Prostitution in Wien* (Vienna, 1925); Coelestin Wolfsgruber, *Joseph O. Cardinal Rauscher* (Freiburg, 1888).

Bruno Grimschitz, *Oesterreichische Maler vom Biedermaier zur Moderne* (Vienna, 1964), Walther Buchowiecki, *Geschichte der Malerei in Wien* (Vienna, 1955), fine illustrations; Karl Ginhart, *Wiener Kunstgeschichte* (Vienna, 1948), short; Richard K. Donin, *Der Wiener Stephansdom* (new ed., Vienna, 1952); Josef Nadler, *Literaturgeschichte Oesterreichs* (new ed., Salzburg, 1951); Hans Kohn, *Karl Kraus, Arthur Schnitzler, Otto Weininger* (Tuebingen, 1962), interpretative.

Paul Vasili (pseud.), *La Société de Vienne* (Paris, 1885); Victor Tissot, *Vienne et la vie Viennoise* (Paris, 1878); Frédéric Kohn-Arbest, *Vienne sous François Joseph 1er* (Paris, 1888), interesting.

≈§ ह≈

Index

Index

Index

The text for Vienna in the Age of Franz Josef *has been set on the Linotype in 10-point Baskerville, with two points of space between lines for added legibility. The paper on which the book is printed bears the watermark of the University of Oklahoma Press and has an effective life of at least three hundred years.*